WORKING WITH
EMBROIDERY
— KITS —

WORKING WITH
EMBROIDERY
— KITS —

HELEN PERKS

CASSELL

Dedication

To Vivian Mead, Sheila Fraser, Jenny Chippendale and Sue Mills who have given me much encouragement and inspiration through their teaching.

A CASSELL BOOK

First published in the UK
1992 by Cassell
Villiers House
41/47 Strand
LONDON
WC2N 5JE

Distributed in the United States
by Sterling Publishing Co., Inc.
387 Park Avenue South, New York, NY 10016-8810

Distributed in Australia
by Capricorn Link (Australia) Pty Ltd
PO Box 665, Lane Cove, NSW 2066

British Library Cataloguing-in-Publication Data
Perks, Helen, *1967–*
    Working with embroidery kits.
    I. Title
    746.44

ISBN 0-304-31435-5

Photography by Campbell MacCallum
except insets on pages 41, 44, 64 and 92

Typeset by Chapterhouse, Formby, L37 3PX
Printed and bound in Singapore
by Craft Print.

Contents

Acknowledgements

I wish to thank everyone who has lent their support to me during the writing of this book, especially during the times when it was not advisable to mention the B.O.O.K. within my earshot; namely Jane Moss who has typed and read the text so many times that she knows it better than I do; Hazel Everett who has worked some of the samples as well as reading the text for technical details; everyone at the Centre for Embroidery, Fashion and Textile Studies, particularly Jenny Fitzgerald-Bond for giving me space to work as well as working some samples, but most of all for their limitless support and advice; Jon Mills who spent many evenings with me editing, shortening my two-hundred-word sentences and supplying wonderful chocolate cookies; my mum and sister Sarah for typing some bits and pieces; Yvonne Yeomanson and Marion Bishop, my contacts in America; and finally Adrian Mudd who photographed some of the samples in their part-worked state.

I would also like to thank the following companies for their generous contributions and support: Cara Ackerman of DMC Creative World; Sarah Harper of Coats Anchor; Jane Rainbow; Beth Russell of Designer Forum; Hanni Davis of Deri Designs; and Pamela Vogel of Ivo Tapestries.

Introduction

Kits are one of the best ways of learning about embroidery. They offer the novice stitcher the opportunity to master a stitch or technique, without having to be concerned with such things as the suitability of the thread to fabric and whether the correct needle has been chosen. The beauty of kits is that everything has been thought through for you; all you have to do is decide on the design you like best. Kits come in varying styles, needing different levels of skill to complete them; many have a scoring level to help you decide. With the increased popularity of embroidery as a hobby there are always new kits to choose from which cater for most tastes and pockets. Many people find that the only thing lacking in these kits are the instructions, which is the reason for this book. It is aimed at people who have done little or no embroidery before, but wish to learn more about the techniques. It is designed as a teaching book, giving instructions on how and where to start a project, as well as how to work some of the more popular stitches. By using this book you will be able to choose the correct equipment for a project and learn how to use it properly. There are also details of the fabrics, threads and needles that are commonly available, so that you can choose your own when you progress to working your own designs. There are chapters on the more popular techniques available in kit form, such as canvas work, cross stitch, crewel work, surface stitchery and silk shading. These chapters contain a potted history and background information on the technique, to give an insight into how embroidery has developed over the centuries. Each chapter then goes on to describe the different types of kits you can find in the shops and so help you choose one you will be capable of working. It also explains, using written instructions and illustrations, how to go about stitching your project, giving hints to help prevent problems.

The chapter on making your own kit gives ideas for designing your own projects and how best to transfer them on to fabric. It also gives ideas for experimenting, using kits, so as to make your finished piece more individual. The final chapter is concerned with finishing and making up your embroidery. These processes are just as important as the actual embroidery and are often overlooked. In fact, many kit instructions do not cover the subject at all.

From the information you pick up from this book I hope you will not only improve your stitching, but have a go at trying new techniques and using different threads and stitches. Embroidery is a vast subject and there is always something new to learn and try out.

However, the most important thing is to enjoy your embroidery. It is a very relaxing hobby that will in turn give you something to admire for many years to come and, like me and many hundreds of others, once you have started you will probably never be able to give it up!

Glossary

Basting The American word for tacking.

Cross-way The cross-way of the fabric is found at a 45° angle to the straight of the grain. Bias cut or true cross are other terms used to describe this cut of fabric. Fabric has greater elasticity along this line.

Interlining The name given to a fabric used to back another fabric of a similar weight to give it more substance and body. Interlining can be woven or non-woven. Some examples are linen holland, linen duck and calico, which are woven. Vilene is a non-woven interlining. Woven interlinings need to be shrunk. This is done by wetting the fabric and then ironing it dry. Always clean your iron afterwards. Washing woven interlining will remove the agent that stiffens the fabric, so leaving it limp and unusable.

Intersection The point where the warp or weft threads go over or under one another, forming a cross.

Napped fabrics These have a definite one-way pile which should always lie in the same direction. Usually you will need to allow extra fabric for this. Velvet is a napped fabric, for instance. Many printed fabrics require extra fabric allowance in the same way, so that the pattern will match.

Pricking A tracing of a design that has had small holes pierced along its outlines.

Right side The front or correct side of the fabric or the side of the stitchery that is going to show.

Selvedges The two edges that run along the length of the fabric as it comes off the roll. These are usually tighter and firmer than the rest of the fabric, as they are the turning point for the weft threads. In embroidery, any selvedge needs to be either cut off or snipped into to release the tension. Pieces of fabric in a kit are likely to have only one selvedge. This selvedge was traditionally placed so that it ran along the left edge of the panel but this is not a strict rule.

Stab stitch A smaller version of running stitch which hardly shows on the right side but is longer on the wrong side.

Stitching line The line you choose to sew along, which is a constant distance from the raw edge.

Straight grain Runs parallel to the selvedge and unless otherwise stated all cutting should be done on the straight of the grain, or the fabric will distort and hang oddly. Always frame up on the straight of the grain.

Warp The threads that run parallel to the selvedge; they run the entire length of the fabric.

Weft The threads that run at a 90° angle to the selvedge (an easy way to remember is that the threads that go right to left are the weft). These are the threads that create the different weave patterns.

Working thread The thread that is in the needle and is being used to stitch.

Wrong side The reverse side of the fabric or stitching; the side which will not show. There is not always a definite wrong side to certain fabrics.

❧ 1 ❧

Choosing the Right Equipment

EMBROIDERY FRAMES

'Should I use a frame?' is a question I am asked time and time again. It is really a matter of personal preference, but there are many advantages to using a frame and I always do. I find it quicker and it is easier to control the stitch tension, so achieving a neater finished piece. Although you may find a frame awkward to use at first, with time and practice you will discover many advantages. There are times, though, when you may not find it practical to use a frame, for example when travelling. This will not be detrimental to your work as long as you take care when stitching. Most distortion can be resolved afterwards with stretching, but lumps and bumps cannot always be removed, so neatness and tension are very important.

Square frames

Square frames come in various sizes and different types including travel frames and slate frames. Travel frames measure approximately 12 in (30 cm) in width and vary in length from 12 in (30 cm) to 36 in (91.5 cm). They have two side arms, usually square, and two rollers made of dowelling with webbing attached along the length (the length of the webbing determines the size of the frame). Once the fabric has been sewn on to the webbing (see chapter 2), the rollers may slot into the gaps at either end of the arms where wing nuts are used to keep them from slipping, or alternatively there will be holes in the arms where the screw shank at the end of the roller can be inserted, and again wing nuts are used. Travel frames cannot be made as taut as slate frames but they are a lot cheaper and are suitable for the beginner or for small panels of embroidery.

Slate frames are a lot stronger than travel frames and are also made of heavier wood, so are more expensive. They consist of two rollers with webbing along the length, and two arms which may either have holes drilled at regular intervals at either end with split pins used to keep the frame taut, or may be cut with a screw thread with discs to keep the frame taut. Some makes of frame use a combination of the two types of arms. These frames come in lengths from 18 in (46 cm) to 36 in (91.5 cm), although larger ones can be ordered. The arms are usually the same length as the frame but this will not be the case with larger frames, for practical reasons.

As slate frames are heavy and bulky, they need to be supported. The best supports are trestles, which can be bought from some furniture shops and embroidery-frame makers. Alternatively you could work in an armchair where the frame could be rested on the arms, or put two chairs back to back, a little less than the width of the frame apart, resting the frame across the top of the chairs. Another way is to attach the frame to the edge of a table with G-clamps, placing some sort of padding between the table top and the wing nuts.

These ways of supporting the frame leave you both hands free to work. You should have one hand beneath the frame and one hand above, usually the right hand underneath for the right-handed, and the left for the left-handed. At first you will find it slower, but with practice it makes working a lot quicker and it will soon become second nature. There are some stitches, however, such as French knots, that require both hands to be above the frame.

You can also buy slate frames that have been adapted to fit into a floor-standing base. These are called floor frames. They are less versatile than a frame and trestles, because with a floor frame only one size of frame can be used.

Ring frames

Ring frames come in sizes from 3½ in (9 cm) to 20 in (51 cm). They can be made of wood or plastic and consist of two rings of the same material which fit together. Larger wooden frames can be bought with a dowel rod and barrel clamp attached which can be clamped to the edge of a table, or used with a floor stand to enable you to work with both hands. Ring frames specially designed for machine embroidery consist of a metal inner and plastic outer ring. They can also be used for hand embroidery. Ring frames should always be bound with fabric tape to prevent damage to the fabric and stitchery.

Which frame should be used?

Square frames are suitable for all types of embroidery but are most commonly used for canvas work as they hold the fabric taut on all sides, and any excess fabric can be kept around the roller without damaging it. Ring frames are suitable for cross stitch, crewel work, silk shading and surface stitchery. Small panels of canvas embroidery can be worked in this way, but only where the whole of the design is enclosed in the ring frame, because the ring will damage the weave of the canvas underneath it, making it unsuitable for stitching. It is important always to remove the embroidery from the ring frame when you are not working to prevent ring marks on both fabric and stitching.

GENERAL SEWING EQUIPMENT

Scissors

For embroidery you will need a small sharp pair of scissors with blades no longer than 4 in (10 cm), as they are easy to control when cutting threads. For the techniques listed in this book the scissors do not need to be very pointed. You will also need a pair of dressmaking shears for trimming around cushions and cutting out fabric. For cutting canvas and paper, use an old pair of shears since these materials tend to blunt the shears quickly. When buying a pair of scissors, always take some thread or fabric along with you to test the cutting action, especially the tips of small scissors.

Thimbles

Thimbles are not absolutely necessary for many types of embroidery. Thimbles are worn on the middle finger and if you are working with a square frame you will need thimbles for both hands. They are made from all sorts of material, such as stainless steel, wood, enamel, silver, china and leather. They come in various sizes so should be tried on to find a comfortable fit. An antique silver thimble can be worth investing in. Many people find them more comfortable and they are also more attractive.

If you find shop-bought thimbles uncomfortable to wear, try making leather ones. These can be particularly useful if you have long fingernails. They are easily made from medium-weight leather, which should be dye-fast. Cut a square that will wrap around your finger and is long enough to come down to the first joint. Fold the square round your finger, then stitch around it with a running stitch so that the leather fits snugly. Remove the thimble and finish off by stitching round it again, trimming off any excess leather. The leather will stretch with use so you may need to take in any excess now and again.

A range of frames and equipment. Standing at the back are a slate frame on the left and a travel frame on the right. In front of these from left to right are three types of ring frame; a barrel clamp ring frame, two machine embroidery ring frames (blue) and two bound wooden ring frames. In the foreground is a selection of general equipment – scissors, thimbles, beeswax, a needle holder and a needle cleaner.

Beeswax

This is used for strengthening thread. It is useful, for example, when you are sewing on beads which can wear the thread. Thread the needle first, and put your finger over the eye. Then pull the loose thread over the block of beeswax, giving the thread a light protective coating.

Needle cleaners

These are usually made in the shape of strawberries and are filled with emery powder. They are used to clean up needles which have rust on them or have turned black with working. The needle is pushed in and out of the pad to clean it. A needle cleaner will not return blackened needles to their original silver colour; it will just make the surface of the needle smoother.

THREADS

The range of threads available changes all the time, as small companies are set up and retail hand-dyed and spun threads. The threads described here are the ones generally available throughout the world.

Stranded cotton

Stranded cotton is probably the most widely used embroidery thread. It is available in a wide range of colours and is usually supplied in cross stitch, silk shading and free surface stitchery kits. Occasionally it is included in canvas kits. It is packed in skeins which if pulled carefully from one end will neatly unravel. If you pull the thread from the wrong end you will feel some resistance. The thread comes as six fine strands slightly twisted together. This thread is very versatile: it can be used as it comes, or by cutting a length you can split the threads into strands. When splitting the thread count the number of strands you require halfway along the length, then run your finger to the end of the length, outwards, so separating the thread. To get rid of any excess twisting, gently run the thread through your fingers. In kits stranded cotton usually comes in pre-cut lengths.

Coton perlé (pearl cotton)

Coton perlé does not come in such an extensive colour range as stranded cotton and is sometimes used in canvas and cross stitch kits. It can be bought in various thicknesses, 3 being the thickest, followed by 5 which is the most commonly available, 8, and 12 which is the finest. 3, 8 and 12 come in even fewer colours, 12 being the hardest to obtain and only available in black, white and écru. Perlé has a high lustre and is termed a round thread because it is round in section. Unlike stranded cotton, it cannot be split. It comes in a skein but some shades are available in 50 g balls. To use a skein first remove the labels, then untwist the skein until it looks like a loop. There is a knot holding it all together; cut through all the threads at this point. Depending on the type of embroidery you are undertaking, you can leave the skein like this or you can cut through it again at the opposite end. This way you will get threads of the same length and they can be kept neat. To use the balls, cut lengths of thread as required.

Soft cotton

Soft cotton has a limited colour range compared to stranded cotton and has become very popular again in recent years. It is used in many long stitch kits, particularly those aimed at children, as it is an easy thread to work with. It is available in one thickness and comes in skeins. Like cotton perlé it is a round thread although it has a matt finish.

Coton à broder

This thread has a very limited colour range and is not always easily available. It is sometimes used in cross stitch and in candlewicking kits. The thread is available in four thicknesses, 12 being the thickest, followed in order by 16, 20 and 25. Like coton perlé, it is a round thread but has a matt finish. It is available only in skeins, which have to be treated like the perlé skeins.

Crewel wool

This is a 2-ply fine worsted wool used in canvas and crewel kits. Depending on the brand, the colour range can be extensive and includes many subdued colours. Small quantities are readily available in skeins, which are used by drawing the yarn from one end like stranded cotton. Many companies also produce a large quantity, or hank, of wool, which may have to be ordered. Hanks should be cut through like perlé skeins, then cut through at the opposite end. Like stranded cotton, crewel wool is a versatile thread. A single strand can be used for fine work and more strands for coarser stitchery.

Tapestry wool

Tapestry wool is a thick yarn like 4-ply knitting wool, and is used in canvas kits. It is less versatile than crewel wool but can be used on large-gauge canvases down to 14-gauge. It is an economical yarn for large projects such as carpets or hangings. While some suppliers specialize in tapestry wool, most companies that make crewel wool also produce tapestry wool in the same colour range, and again it is available in skeins and hanks. In some brands, a wide colour range may be available in skeins, with selected shades coming only in hanks. The wool can be used in the same way as crewel wool.

Threads. Top row from left to right:
Coton à broder, stranded cotton, soft
cotton and coton perlé. Bottom row
from left to right: crewel wool, tapestry
wool and Persian wool.

Fabrics

1. *Single or mono canvas*
2. *Interlock canvas*
3. *Sudan rug canvas*
4. *Double or Penelope canvas*
5. *Aida*
6. *Easy-count aida*
7. *Evenweave linen*
8. *Linen twill*
9. *Cotton sateen.*

Persian wool

This is stranded wool which comes as three strands together, giving a thickness similar to tapestry wool. When split, it is a little thicker than crewel wool. Persian wool is a high quality yarn made from virgin wool and is used in some canvas kits and many crewel kits. It is bought in skeins which are used like crewel wool skeins and very large hanks can be ordered.

FABRICS

Canvas

Modern canvas is made up of threads, usually cotton, woven to form a grid structure. (The thread also has a glue/resin finish which when wetted resets the canvas: see chapter 8.) This grid is used as the basis for embroidery which hides the canvas completely. It is available in different sizes which are termed the gauge or mesh. The gauge is defined by the number of threads to the inch; canvas gauges range from 3 to 25. For finer work, silk gauze or fine double canvas may be suitable. These are often used as the basis for embroideries for doll's houses. Canvas comes in various widths, qualities and colours.

Single or mono canvas

This type of canvas, as its name suggests, is woven with a single thread, in the usual over/under weave. It comes in various qualities, widths and colours. Different names are used to describe the qualities in which single canvas is available. French is thought to be the best, followed by deluxe, more easily obtainable than French but still of a high quality. Lower qualities are also produced. Most types are available in either white or antique and some of the finer canvases are also available in pastel colours. Single canvas comes in gauges 10 to 24.

Interlock canvas

This type of canvas looks at first sight like single canvas. The weft thread, however, instead of going over and under, pierces the warp thread. Most printed kits are worked on this type of canvas. Interlock canvas is not of as good quality as single canvas. Care must be taken when working not to cause too much distortion, as interlock does not always go back into shape. Interlock comes only in white, in gauges 10 to 18. Sudan rug canvas is also an interlock canvas available in cream and in gauges 4 to 7.

Double or Penelope canvas

The threads of this type of canvas are woven like mono canvas, but in pairs. Double canvas is useful for working designs with detailed areas and coarser work on the same panel. This is called pricking the ground, and is done by running the point of the needle down between the pairs of threads, so that you turn part of the canvas into mono canvas, while the majority of the stitchery will be worked over the double threads. When stitching over double canvas, treat the pairs as if they were single canvas. The canvas is available in antique and white and in gauges 7 to 20; this actually means that there are between 14 and 40 threads to the inch.

Evenweave fabric

This fabric is normally made of linen or cotton and the threads are woven at an even distance apart, so that there are the same number of threads to the inch in both directions. It is similar to canvas, but the threads are closer together and much softer. The threads should not have too many slubs or flaws, although linen evenweave does have quite a few slubs due to the nature of the flax fibre. Evenweave is used for counted thread techniques like cross stitch. It is available in a variety of colours, including dark and pastel shades and the gauges go from 14 to 36.

Aida and binca

Aida is a cotton fabric and the weave consists of fine threads, interlocking to create definite square holes. Binca is the name given to the very large-gauge versions of this fabric. Aida and binca are easier to count than evenweave, making them ideal fabrics for beginners. They are available in a wide range of colours and come in gauges 8 to 22. An easy-count aida is now available, which has a fine grey thread running through every tenth block. This thread is removed after stitching. Easy-count is available only in white and cream and in 11, 14 and 18 gauges.

Linen twill

Twill refers to the type of weave which goes diagonally across the width. When using twill, the diagonal should go from the bottom left to the top right corner. Linen twill was traditionally used for crewel work and is usually beige or natural-coloured.

Cotton sateen

The majority of crewel wool kits now use sateen rather than twill. On the right side it has a smooth satin finish and on the wrong side it is a plain weave.

NEEDLES

In embroidery it is important to use the correct needle for the technique. The wrong needle could cause the thread to wear or create large, unsightly holes in the fabric.

Once you have chosen the correct type of needle, you then need to find the right size. A needle should pass through the fabric without leaving huge holes, but it should also take the thread through the fabric without causing wear.

Tapestry needles

These needles have blunt points and an elongated eye, to make the threading of thick yarns easier. They are used for canvas and counted thread work, like cross stitch, because the blunt point does not split the threads of the fabric. Tapestry needles come in sizes from 13, the largest, to 26, the smallest.

Chenille needles

These look like tapestry needles but have a sharp point. They are used for solid fabrics like twill and for thicker threads that are not suitable for crewel needles. Chenille needles come in sizes 18 to 26.

Crewel needles

These look like general sewing needles, which are referred to as sharps. However, crewel needles have a large eye to take embroidery threads. They come in a size range from 1 to 10, 10 being the finest.

Beading needles

As the name suggests, these are used for sewing down beads. They are very long thin needles and bend easily, so may not be suitable for all fabrics used in embroidery. The number 10 crewel needle can be used instead.

Curved needles

These are not actually used in embroidery but in the making up processes described in the book. They come in various sizes and are sometimes called mattress needles. The sizes are determined by the measurement of the curve: for example, a size 8 has a curve 8 cm long. A size 5 is the most useful in the making up process.

Embroidery needles showing different sizes.

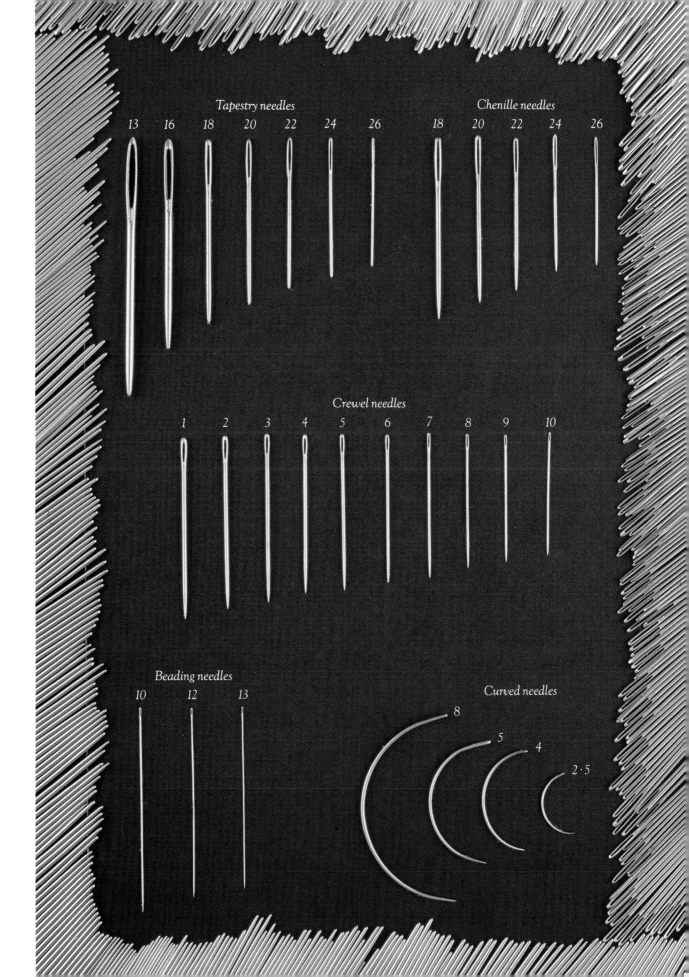

Tapestry needles
13 16 18 20 22 24 26

Chenille needles
18 20 22 24 26

Crewel needles
1 2 3 4 5 6 7 8 9 10

Beading needles
10 12 13

Curved needles
8 5 4 2·5

❧ 2 ❧

Before You Begin

For beginners I would recommend a small piece like a pincushion or a small picture. This will allow you to learn the basics of a technique, but can be completed quickly. You will learn fast by completing a small piece first, then going on to bigger projects once you have found a technique that you enjoy. Embroidery *can* be very expensive, but it need not be. Not only do kits come in a wide range of styles, but they also vary in price from a few pounds or dollars up to hundreds. The most important thing to bear in mind when you are buying a kit is the design. You will find embroidery a far more pleasant experience if you like what you are working on. There is an enormous variety of kits on the market now, so there should be something for everyone.

If you wish to start with canvas work, avoid hand-painted designs. They are not widely available and because of the hand work involved in producing them are very expensive. The shading on them is also very detailed and a daunting task for a beginner. A hand-painted panel is a challenge and needs to be worked in a good light. It is definitely not for working while sitting in front of the television. The best designs for a novice are ones that use blocks of colour. Many manufacturers state the skill level required for working a particular kit. This is a very useful guide when choosing your first piece. Try to avoid designs that are to be stitched on fine canvas; a 14-gauge or coarser are ideal. The majority of kits are worked on 14-gauge, so this will not greatly limit your choice.

When choosing a cross stitch design there are few limitations for beginners. For charted designs, a kit based on aida will make counting easier. Designs that contain a lot of unconnected motifs, like some of the Dutch samplers, are best avoided. Printed cross stitch designs are very simple to follow, as the stitch is made over the printed crosses. Some of these kits may also incorporate other stitches such as satin stitch.

Crewel, silk shading and free surface stitchery kits vary very little in the amount of experience necessary. Many of the stitches used in these techniques – particularly long-and-short shading – require practice to achieve a neat finish, so do not expect perfection the first time round. If you find a stitch difficult to do, it can always be replaced with one that you find easier.

PREPARATION

Depending on the technique you have chosen, there will be various preparations that need to be undertaken before starting the actual embroidery. These processes should not be overlooked. A few minutes at the beginning may save hours later on, as well as helping to give a better finish to your work.

When you have bought your kit check the contents. Most kits have a list of what they should contain. A rough guide to what should be in a kit is as follows:

Canvas work

In printed kits there will be a piece of canvas with your chosen design printed on it and sufficient thread to complete the design. The background thread may not be included. For charted designs there will be a piece of blank canvas, threads and a chart with the design plotted on it. With outlined designs, the outline will be printed on to the canvas. There will be a drawing of the design to show which stitches and colours go where, plus of course the threads. If you are not using a frame then it is important to tape the raw edges of the canvas with masking tape. This prevents it from fraying or snagging your clothes.

Cross stitch

Cross stitch kits will contain similar materials to the canvas kits, except that fabric will replace the canvas. When the design is printed on to the fabric it will not be in colour, as with canvas. There will be an illustration to denote the use of colour. The threads will usually be supplied in pre-cut lengths. To prevent the fabric from fraying, either turn under a hem or alternatively zigzag-stitch the raw edges on a sewing machine.

Crewel work, silk shading and free surface stitchery

The design may already appear on the fabric as an outline, or there will be an iron-on transfer. To denote colour and stitch usage there will be an illustration, and there will also be a bundle of threads. The fabric in these kits will need neatening in the same way as for cross stitch kits.

All kits contain working instructions, some better than others. There will be a needle of the correct size and type. Most kits do not contain the materials to make them into the item that may be shown in the photograph; this will often be just a guide to how you could use your finished piece.

Having opened the kit, the next step is to sort out the threads. Many kits now contain what is termed a multi-skein. This is a skein of threads cut to the same length but of different colours. Separate them, so that you have a bundle of each shade. If the kits contains skeins of threads and there are several of the same shade, stick them together with sticky tape along the labels. Also, so that you know which colour is which, cut off a small piece of each and tape it to the label. Then, if you run out of a shade, you will know its name and code number.

Down the side of many printed canvas kits are small squares showing each shade used in the design. Cut off a short length of each shade and tie it through the appropriate square. Adjacent colours printed on a design can sometimes be difficult to identify, as they can be affected by surrounding colours that make them look quite different from the sample squares. You may also find that the colours vary quite a lot from the appropriate thread colour, to make it easier to follow the design.

In other types of kits there will be a colour key corresponding to the symbols used on the chart or illustration. There may be a cardboard palette in the pack, in which case you should label each hole with a symbol and thread through the appropriate colour of yarn. If there is no palette, either make your own or label each shade with its correct symbol.

Illustrations for kits that use different stitches will use a symbol for each stitch. They may look a little complicated, but they are really quite simple to understand if followed carefully.

USING AN IRON-ON TRANSFER

Cut off anything printed on your transfer that you do not want to appear on your panel. Set your iron to the wool setting without steam for single-impression transfers and cotton for multi-print ones (these are usually printed in silver).

Place the ready-pressed fabric on a smooth flat surface large enough to take the transfer area. Place the transfer in the required position, print side down, on the right side of the fabric. Pin each corner to prevent the transfer from moving, but do not place the iron on the pins or they will mark the fabric. Apply the iron for a few seconds. If the transfer is small, protect the surrounding fabric by covering it with tissue paper. Carefully lift one corner to see if the design has taken. If not, repeat the process, but be careful not to move the transfer or you will end up with a double impression. Once you are sure it has taken, carefully peel off the transfer.

FRAMING UP

This is the term used to describe putting the fabric on to a square frame. Another term is 'dressing the frame'. The whole idea of using a frame is to keep the fabric taut and straight to help prevent distortion. It is important that the fabric is sewn in on the straight of the grain.

Materials needed

A square frame   The length of the frame must be large enough to take one edge of the fabric to be embroidered. It is preferable to have the design running parallel to the rollers. This will give you a better idea of how the panel is progressing, and the stitches will be going in the correct direction. Traditionally, any selvedge should run along the left-hand side of the design, but this is not always the case with printed canvases in kits.

Upholstery webbing

Button thread

Pins

String

A number 13 tapestry needle   or a needle large enough to take the string

1 Turn under a single hem of ⅜ in (1 cm) on two opposite sides of the fabric to be embroidered. These edges will be stitched to the webbing on the rollers and are usually the top and bottom edges of the fabric.

2 Measure and mark the central point of the frame and the webbing. Do the same along the turned-over edge of the fabric.

3 Put the wrong side of the fabric and the webbing together, pinning the centre points. Pull the webbing and fabric taut and keep them edge to edge. Pin along the length of the webbing and remember that the pins should go in vertically, and that you should pin from the centre outwards so as to ease the webbing down the fabric evenly.

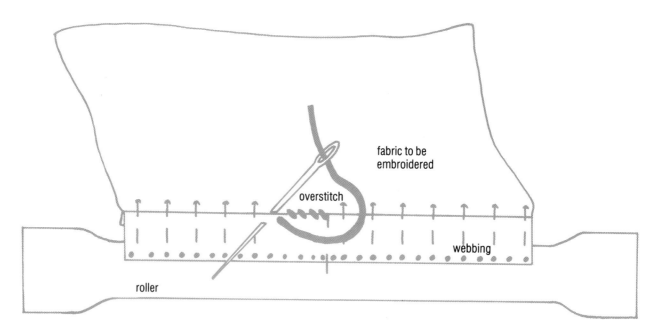

Fig. 1 *Framing up. Turn under a small hem, then pin the fabric to the webbing, aligning the centre marks. Overstitch the two together and fasten off securely.*

4 Using the button thread single in the needle, sew the webbing and the fabric together. Start in the centre, putting the knot between the fabric and the webbing. Sew from the centre towards the outside edge, using fairly small overstitches about ³⁄₁₆ in (3 mm) long. Remember that although these stitches have to keep the fabric on the frame, they also have to be unpicked at a later date. When finishing off the thread, stitch back over the last five or so stitches, forming a sort of cross stitch.

5 Repeat the process on the opposite side, using the other roller.

6 Put the frame together. Roll in any excess fabric, so that the centre of the design is visible. With larger frames, make sure that you can comfortably reach the centre without stretching too much. The frame should be as taut as possible.

7 To help keep the fabric taut and to pull it from all sides, upholstery webbing needs to be stitched down the sides. Pin the webbing so that it is half on the fabric and half off and follows one of the vertical grain lines. Stitch the webbing on to the side of the fabric using a diagonal tacking stitch in single button thread. Do not make the stitches any wider than ½ in (13 mm) or longer than ¾ in (2 cm).

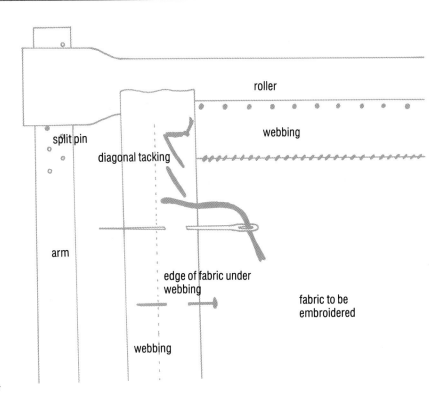

Fig. 2 *Detail of framing up showing diagonal tacking. The webbing needs to be half on the edge of the fabric and half off.*

8 Using the large tapestry needle, take the string down through the webbing and around the arms at 1¼ in (3 cm) intervals. When you have string down both sides, tie it off at one end and tighten it, making sure that both sides are equal. Then tie off the other ends. The string, like the frame, will need tightening from time to time.

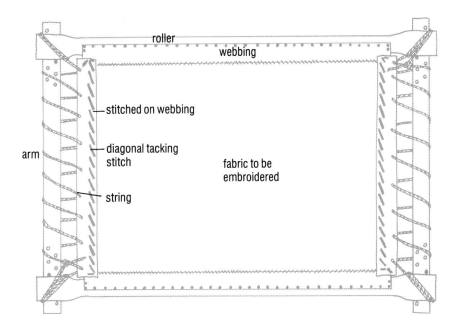

Fig. 3 *Square frame ready to be worked on. The fabric should be taut with no wrinkles. For long pieces of embroidery it will be necessary to roll the excess round the rollers.*

9 On travel frames there is not always enough room to get webbing down the sides, and since travel frames are rolled on quite frequently, it is not always convenient to have string and webbing down the sides. Another method of pulling the fabric at the the sides, which is really suitable only for short-term use, is to use either string or 1 in (2.5 cm) cotton tape. Instead of stitching the string through the webbing, put a pin through the edge of the fabric and then anchor the string around it. When using tape, pin through the tape. Pull the fabric taut as you go. These methods will not keep the fabric as taut as the webbing and string method.

Fig. 4 *Framing up with pins and string. Put the pin through the fabric first, then loop the string around it. Tie off the excess string at either end of the frame.*

Fig. 5 *Framing up with pins and cotton tape. Tie off one end of the tape, take it across to the fabric and pin it. Then go round the frame and repeat.*

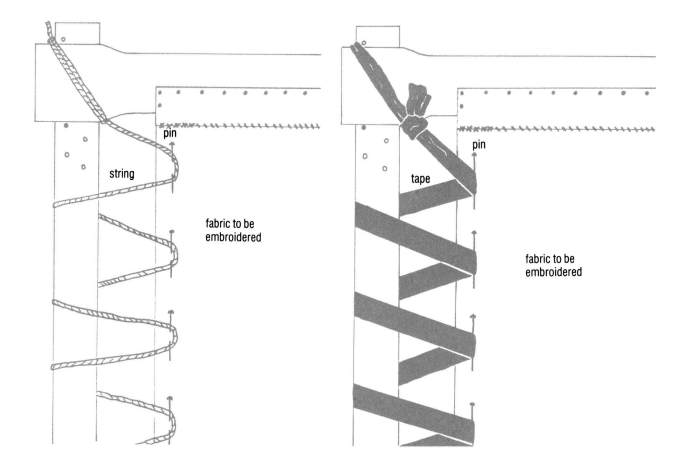

10 For fine fabrics such as linen and silk, another method can be used. This is done before stitching the fabric on to the roller. Make sure that the edges are cut on the straight of the grain. Cut a piece of string the length of the fabric where the webbing and the string would normally go. Turn over about ½ in (13 mm) of fabric, enclosing the string, then stitch very close to the string using a small, secure running stitch. Frame up in the normal way, but stitch the string through the fabric so that it is pulling against the enclosed string.

Fig. 6 *Framing up with string down the sides. This method is suitable for fine fabrics. The string must be enclosed down the sides before the fabric is sewn on to the rollers.*

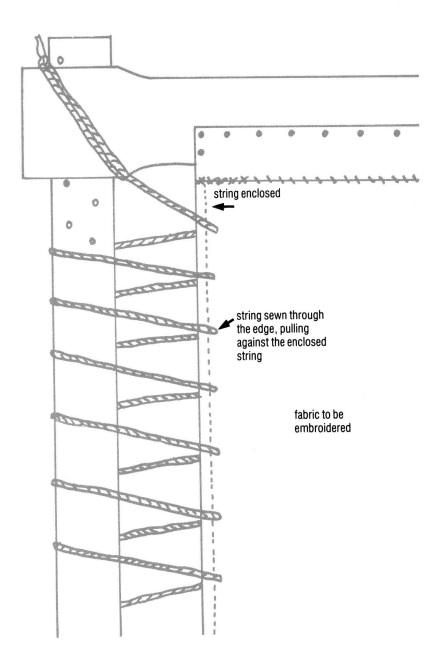

string enclosed

string sewn through the edge, pulling against the enclosed string

fabric to be embroidered

BINDING A RING FRAME

With wooden ring frames, which I prefer for both durability and stability, it is important to bind the outer hoop before starting to stitch. This will help keep the fabric taut in the frame while working, and will prevent ring marks and snagging of the fabrics on any bits of rough wood. This is particularly important since the outer hoop goes against the right side of the fabric. There are some ring frames currently on the market that claim to need no binding, and some of the plastic and metal and plastic types cannot be bound.

There are some types of fabric such as velvet and canvas that will mark whether the frame is bound or not. For these fabrics, use a square frame or no frame at all. If you are using a light-coloured fabric, you can put a piece of tissue paper over the right side of the fabric to be embroidered, place it in the frame, then tear away the tissue paper in the area where the design is to be worked. This helps to stop grease from your hands getting on to the fabric. For lightweight fabrics like organza, bind the inner frame as well as the outer one. Always remove the fabric from the ring frame when you are not stitching. This will minimize damage to the fabric.

Materials needed

Cotton tape   or fabric torn into strips no wider than 1 in (2.5 cm)
A ring frame   It should be large enough to contain the whole design or a very large part of it, so that it is not necessary to have the ring over any part of the stitching, which can be damaged by the frame

1   Start off by wrapping the tape around the outer hoop of the frame, binding over the end a couple of times to prevent it from coming undone.

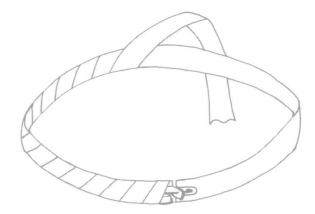

Fig. 7 *Binding a ring frame. Bind the outer hoop with cotton tape to prevent ring marks. For very delicate fabrics it may be necessary to bind the inner hoop.*

2   Continue to bind the frame by overlapping the tape about ½ in (13 mm) or half the width of the tape, whichever is least. Go round the whole hoop like this.

3   To finish off, fold under a small amount of tape so that it will end on the outer edge of the hoop, then stitch over securely. Once you have bound your ring frame you will need to re-do it only when the tape becomes dirty.

4   To use a ring frame, place the fabric over the inner hoop. Then place the outer hoop on top and push down on to the inner hoop, trapping the fabric. The fabric needs to be taut and can be tightened by gently pulling the fabric on its straight of grain to avoid distortion. The fabric may also need to be tightened during working.

FOLLOWING A CHART

Charts can seem very daunting at first sight, with all their different colours and symbols and a blank piece of fabric in front of you. However there are a few steps that can be taken to make matters a little easier. Once you get started using these guidelines, you should find that following a chart is no longer a problem. You may find that not all these tips apply to you, so use the ones that do.

1   Your chart may already be enlarged but, if not, it can easily be done on a photocopier. If the chart is in a book, photocopying will help preserve it.

2   If the chart is not in colour, lightly colour it in. This makes it easier to recognize the shades quickly.

3   After working a small section, lightly cross off this area with a pencil. The marks can be rubbed out later if you wish to reuse the chart.

4   If it is a large chart, counting can be made easier by making every tenth line darker. This is particularly helpful when there are a lot of open spaces.

5   Remember that each square on the chart represents an intersection in the fabric, which in turn becomes a stitch.

6   On the fabric, tack in the centre lines on the vertical and horizontal. Use a pale colour so that when the threads are removed there will be no marks. On canvas, the lines can be drawn on using a HB or 2B pencil. Never use a ballpoint pen or felt pen, unless it is designed for canvas embroidery and is completely waterproof.

7   Always mark the centre lines or the central stitch on the chart.

8   Always start in the centre as this will ensure that the design fits onto the fabric.

When using a charted design always start from the centre and work outwards from that point, so mark the central stitch on the chart and tack in the centre lines horizontally and vertically. These will be removed when the project is complete. Make every tenth line darker on the chart, and, with a pencil, mark off the areas you have finished. The photograph shows a chart, a part-worked piece of the design and the finished piece.

GENERAL HINTS FOR EMBROIDERY

1   Always start at the centre of the design, working outwards from that point.

2   Do not use lengths of thread over 18 in (46 cm) because as you stitch, the thread gets worn by the fabric. It will then lose its lustre and become uneven, giving your work a dull and patchy look. When working on fabric with a very large gauge you will have to use a longer length in order to avoid frequently rethreading your needle. Likewise, for very fine fabrics you will need shorter lengths.

3   As you stitch you may find that the thread twists. This will make your work look uneven, as the thread appears finer when it twists and will not cover the fabric as well. So every now and again let your needle and thread drop below your work, letting it spin back to its natural twist.

4   Do not let your thread become too short when stitching because it makes finishing off difficult and the thread is more likely to have a worn and fluffy look from being in the needle.

5   After unpicking an area discard the thread, unless it is only a couple of stitches. This helps to keep the work looking fresh.

6   Do not rub your work, even though there is a great temptation to do so. It will make it look grubby, and wool embroidery will become fluffy.

7   Always keep your work covered when not stitching, to keep it clean.

8   Always wash your hands before starting to sew, especially when working with light colours.

9   Do not lean or rest on your frame as you will stretch your fabric and cause distortion.

10   Do not wear fluffy jumpers when working, as you will find that fibres get into the stitching and are virtually impossible to remove.

11   Never have tea, coffee or anything that can spill on to or mark your work near to hand.

12   Working in a good light is very important, not only for your stitching but also for your eyesight.

❧ 3 ❧

Canvas Work

Canvas work is made by stitching through a mesh-type fabric called canvas which comes in different types and gauges. It is probably the most popular type of embroidery, and is frequently but wrongly referred to as tapestry. When tent stitch is worked on the finer types of canvas it does resemble tapestry, but real tapestry is in fact worked on a loom. Other and correct terms used to denote this type of work are needlepoint, *gros point* and *petit point*. The latter two names refer to the size of stitch. *Gros point* is the larger stitch worked on double canvas and *petit point* is the name given to the smaller stitch used for detailed areas on double canvas.

Canvas work is a historic technique and was very popular during the late seventeenth and early eighteenth centuries, when biblical stories were depicted in embroidered panels, worked on very fine canvas. The characters were all dressed in costumes of the period. Some very good examples of such work can be found in the textile study room of London's Victoria & Albert Museum. Canvas work was brought back into fashion by the Victorians who used it for almost everything, from bags and cushions to men's braces. During the latter part of the nineteenth century chemical aniline dyes were invented, making available a new and vibrant colour range. The dyes were employed in the manufacture in Germany of a soft round wool which was used in a technique called Berlin woolwork. It was extremely popular and the charts were very much in demand. They were some of the first commercially produced patterns and kits. The stitch most commonly used for canvas work is tent stitch. Continental (basketweave) tent stitch is a type of tent stitch which gives exactly the same effect on the right side of the work but is different on the reverse (see page 56). The stitch is made by passing the needle diagonally over the intersection of the warp and weft threads of the canvas. The gauge of the canvas dictates the size of the stitch. There are many other stitches that can be used in canvas work, and that will create texture and depth in your work. The use of a different stitch for the background can make the piece look more interesting and many of the other stitches will also cover the canvas more quickly. A little experimentation can give surprising results.

TYPES OF CANVAS KITS

Hand painted or printed
In these kits the design is already on the canvas as a complete picture. The threads have to be matched with the printed colour and then the print is worked over. The background colour may not be printed and there may be no background colour included in the kit.

Charted
There will be no design on the canvas; instead the design will be plotted on squared paper. The chart may have a symbol code system or may be in colour.

Tramé
These kits are worked on double canvas and at first glance it looks as if the design has already been worked. Lengths of crewel wool are laid horizontally along the canvas, going between the double threads. Sometimes detailed areas like hands and faces are worked in *petit point* on the split canvas.

Traced outline
The design is just an outline on the canvas. This way of transferring the design on to the canvas is quite common when stitches other than tent stitch are used, or for long-stitch kits.

STARTING OFF
Before starting on your kit, especially if you have never done canvas embroidery, it is a good idea to practise the stitches you are going to use. This can be done on the excess fabric around your design (do not cut this excess off) or on a piece of canvas of the same type and gauge as

your kit. This will give you the opportunity to improve your stitching and enable you to calculate the number of strands to use. Remember that everyone's stitch tension is different and that you may require a different amount of thread from that stated on the kit details. Different stitches also require different weights of thread, which need to be tried and tested.

To start, thread your needle. Do this by holding it in your right hand (left, if left-handed) with the point upwards. Fold the thread over this end. Using the thumb and forefinger of the opposite hand, hold the thread tightly wrapped around the needle. Slide the needle out and ease the folded end through the eye, then make a knot at the opposite

Fig. 8 *Starting off for canvas work using the knot and loop methods. So that the embroidery does not have to be turned over, all starting off is done on the right side. The knot will be cut off when the stitchery has entrapped the thread on the wrong side. The loop method can only be used with an even number of threads.*

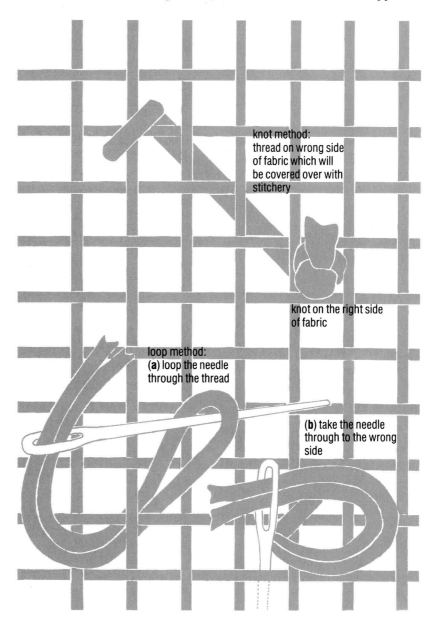

knot method:
thread on wrong side of fabric which will be covered over with stitchery

knot on the right side of fabric

loop method:
(a) loop the needle through the thread

(b) take the needle through to the wrong side

end of the thread. Take the needle through the canvas from the right side to the wrong side, about 1 in (2.5 cm) away from the first area to be worked. Place this thread so that it lies at an angle across the back of the work. This will create a more even effect on the front. When you are a few stitches away from the knot and the thread has been worked over on the wrong side, gently pull the knot so that it is slightly raised above the canvas and snip it off. The thread will then spring back to the wrong side of the canvas, so you will not be left with tufts on the right side.

Another method of starting off is by using a loop. You can use this method only when you require an even number of threads to cover the canvas. First cut your thread twice as long as you require, but this must always be an even number, or you will not be able to have a loop at the end of each thread. The following explanation is for two threads. Put the two ends together so that the opposite end makes a loop. Thread the ends through the needle, checking they are level. Take the needle through the canvas from the right side to the wrong where you wish to start, pulling the thread through and leaving the loop on the right side.

Fig. 9 *Finishing off by weaving the thread through the back of the canvas stitches. When there is no unworked area left, the thread must be taken through the back of the last stitches, going in two directions so that it is secure.*

Take the needle back through the loop, then pull the thread and take the needle back down through the same hole. Give the thread a little tug and the loop will go through to the other side. Continue stitching in the normal way.

FINISHING OFF

To finish off, bring the needle up into an area that is going to be worked, about 1 in (2.5 cm) away from the last area you worked. The thread will then be secured by the next lot of stitches you complete. Do not bring colours into opposing areas that are either very dark or light, or fibres will come through and give a dirty appearance. Do not take the thread across the back of already worked areas; instead, weave it through the back of the existing stitches. This helps to keep the back of the work tidy. When the thread is secured, and you are a few stitches away, snip the end off. There will be times when there are no more spaces that the needle and thread can be brought up into. On these occasions it will be necessary to finish the thread on the wrong side. Take the needle through to the wrong side, then weave the needle through the back of the last lot of stitches. Do this in two different directions to make it very secure, then cut off any excess thread.

HINTS FOR CANVAS WORK

One of the most important rules in canvas work is to take the needle up and down through the canvas rather than scooping it (that is, completing a whole stitch in one movement). This helps to prevent too much distortion of the canvas and wear on the yarn.

Owing to the fact that the canvas is a grid, it is impossible to get perfect curves as you can in surface and free embroidery. So when you wish to stitch a circle, especially if it is small, you will get a stepped outline or a square block. This stepping or disjointed look is very noticeable on large canvas gauges but it is characteristic of canvas work and no fault of your stitching. Many people try to compensate for it by changing the direction of the stitches so that they follow the printed lines. This will only result in a messy and rough-looking piece of stitching.

Note that tent stitch should always go from bottom left of the canvas to top right. When you stitch a circle in a single row of tent stitch you will notice that from 12 o'clock to 3 o'clock and from 6 o'clock to 9 o'clock the stitches will look disjointed. However from 3 o'clock to 6 o'clock and from 9 o'clock to 12 o'clock the stitches will form a straight line on the diagonal.

In many kits you may find that you use a colour to work only a few stitches – when stitching dots, for example. It is not necessary to finish off the thread for each dot, as long as they are no more than 1 in (2.5 cm) apart. This is because too much travelling across the back, particularly in one area, will create bulk on the back of the work, and this in turn will produce an uneven finish on the right side. This also applies to starting and finishing off. Furthermore never take a thread across an area that has already been worked; instead weave the thread through the back of the existing stitches. If you plan your direction of working, however, this should not be a problem. Try to arrange your stitching in such a way that you complete the largest area possible without needing to travel across the back of the stitches.

Another problem that may occur is tufts of thread of a different shade coming through to the front. This can be prevented by, wherever possible, bringing the needle up through the canvas (wrong side to right) in an empty hole and going down in a used one. It can also be prevented by not taking threads for starting or finishing off into areas that are considerably lighter or darker.

Many people worry about the back of their work, thinking that it should be as neat as the front. It is impossible for your work to be as neat on the back, as all your starting and finishing off threads are worked on this side. It is much more important that your work should look good on the front. Remember that the back will never be seen! It should not be lumpy, however, as this will affect the front.

If you are not going to use a frame you may find that your work will distort, but this can be rectified later by stretching. As with all types of embroidery, it is necessary to keep an even tension, so that your finished piece does not look lumpy and uneven. You should not have to tug the thread, as this can make large unsightly holes, but on the other hand the thread should not be loose. Your tension can be affected if there are too many or too few strands in the needle. When there are too many the stitches will look overcrowded, messy and uneven and with some stitches you will completely lose the pattern. With too few strands, you may compensate by leaving the thread too loose so that you can cover the canvas, or the canvas will show through because you are not stitching correctly. If the piece is a cushion or rug it will then wear out a lot more quickly.

Although the kit will provide you with only one needle, you will find it quicker if you have a needle per shade. This is extremely useful when doing shading.

When you have finished your embroidery, check it for missed stitches, before making up. This can easily be done by holding the work up to the light.

A detail showing tent stitch being worked over a printed design. On printed canvas it is not always easy to decide which colour goes where. As a guide, when there is a dominant colour on the canvas intersection, then that is the colour to use. Always work the areas in the foreground and centre of the design first. Never scoop through the canvas with the needle, always go up and down in two separate movements, as this causes less distortion.

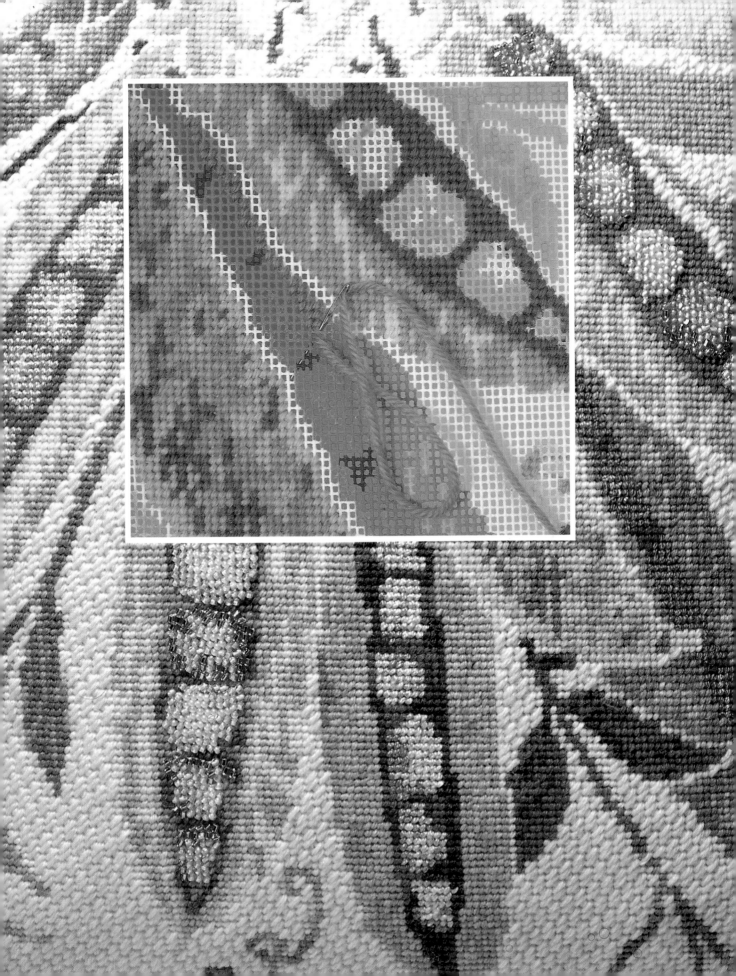

Working a painted or printed design

If the design you have chosen is a naturalistic one, you will need to look and see what object is in the centre of the panel. When you have determined this, visualize this object as being three-dimensional. The part of the object which is nearest to you, in other words in the foreground, is the area where you start.

If the design is stylized or geometric, the same guidelines apply. There may not be an obvious object in the foreground, however, so the choice of where to start must be yours.

So the basic guidelines for the working of a printed design are:

- Work from the centre outwards.
- What's in the foreground and in the centre of the panel?
- Work back into the design.
- The background comes last.

When you have decided where to start, work that area only. First work any outlines or details. Then, working areas in the foreground first with the appropriate colours, stitch that area. After completion go on to the adjacent area and continue like this until the whole object is completed. Then move on to the next.

Never work one colour throughout the design before putting in the next, as this will only give your work a disjointed look. Nor should you work the design as if you were knitting, in rows the whole width of the design from the bottom up. This will make your work very bulky. The only time it is acceptable to use one colour all over a certain area is in designs made up of small blocks of colours, but do not be tempted to travel across the back for more than 1 in (2.5 cm) between blocks.

With printed kits, the type of shading just described is called block shading. As the name suggests, the colours are printed in blocks with no overlapping. If you wish to get a more naturalistic shading, without such hard, obvious colour changes, you can use a method called tweeding. Tweeding can be done only with crewel or Persian wool or stranded cotton and only when more than one strand is used in the needle. This is so that you can use two similar shades together, creating another shade that can be used to break up the changeover line and give a softer look to the design. Start by working your first shade, then when you are one row away from the next shade introduce the mixed one. Work this for a couple of rows, then work the next shade. You can also use it in the background to create a shadow.

Sometimes with printed kits, because the design has not been counted, you may find that features do not lie squarely, or join up where they are supposed to. When this happens you will have to ignore the printed lines and continue the design by counting so that it matches

Fig. 10 *Working order for canvas work on a printed design. Work the vein in the petal first, then work back into the design.*

up. Outlines are also sometimes printed unevenly, even though they should be a single row of stitches.

Another problem is what to do when you have two colours bordering one another. Often it is not obvious which colour should be worked. I make it a rule to use whatever colour is more prominent on the intersection of the canvas. Sometimes this can create odd shapes, however, in which case unpick and use the other colour.

Working a charted design

To make a chart easier to follow, use the guidelines in chapter 2.

Before you start stitching, mark the centre lines on the canvas and chart. Begin stitching from the centre and move outwards, working the design first and then the background. Unlike printed kits, all the detailed work such as shading is already planned, so you do not have to work out what needs to be done first. Stitching outlines first (if there are any) can help in getting the basic design down. It is important to check your counting, because your design could come out an odd shape or not fit the canvas. Dots and small details can be worked before or after the main areas. If you are going to stitch them afterwards, remember to leave the correct amount of space and to weave the threads under the previous stitches. As with printed designs, the background should be worked last.

Bargello, florentine or flame stitch

All of the above names are used to describe this type of work, which was very popular in the early eighteenth century and was used to cover furniture as well as cushions and fashion accessories. This style of work is based on a straight stitch, usually over four threads that are stepped to create points and curves. The rows are normally repeated, using a sequence of colours. It is a very quick technique and once the first row is completed there is very little counting to do. There are many patterns, some more complicated than others, and the pattern can also be split across the diagonal. This is called four-way bargello and gives a sort of kaleidoscope look to the embroidery.

It should always be worked on mono/single or interlock canvas and preferably on canvas no coarser than 14-gauge. A stranded wool gives a superior finish, as it will lie flatter and cover the canvas well. An extra strand can be added if the canvas does show through.

To start work, mark the centre lines as for charted designs. This is because the bargello pattern is also charted and the first row needs to be started in the centre and worked outwards. If you start at the edge or in the corner, the pattern will not balance or look central. Once you have stitched the first row and checked that the counting is correct, the

A detail showing tweeding (left). This is a term which describes a technique used traditionally in canvas shading, where more than one shade or colour is used in the needle, so creating another shade. In this detail two very different colours have been used.

Bargello is based on a straight stitch, usually over four threads, which is stepped to create points and curves. The rows are normally repeated, using a sequence of colours. The photograph (right) shows at the top a very basic pattern, which has then been used to create the four-way bargello pattern at the bottom, which gives a kaleidoscope effect.

subsequent lines follow on, working through the colour sequence. When you are working these lines, either the upper or lower edge of the stitches goes into the same hole as the previous row, so that no canvas shows. When you get to the upper or lower edge of your panel you will need to do incomplete stitches, to make a straight line. To start and finish off, use the instructions for canvas work but leave 1½ in (4 cm) instead of 1 in (2.5 cm) to make sure that the thread is worked in. This is because straight stitches do not hold the starting and finishing off threads as securely as stitches such as tent stitch.

Fig. 11 *A simple bargello pattern. There are many patterns for bargello, some quite complicated, but using exciting colours will make the simplest of patterns look striking.*

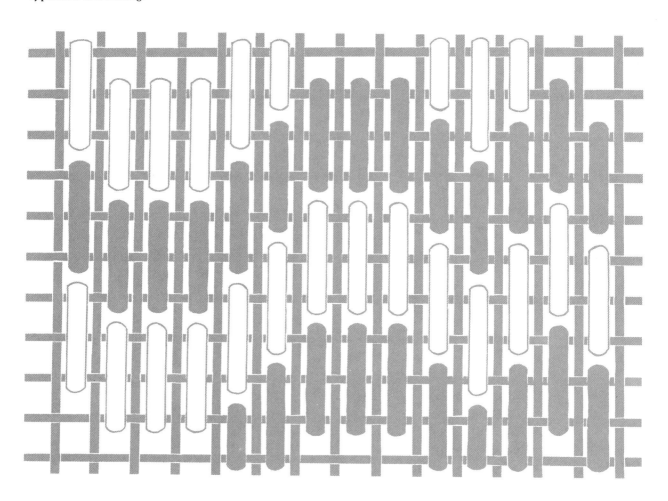

Four-way bargello

All bargello patterns can be used to work a four-way design. The pattern is worked in lines, but the stitches are turned 90° along a diagonal dividing line. This dividing line leaves a definite seam line and the pattern converges at this point, creating interesting effects.

To work four-way bargello you first need to mark your canvas. Mark the centre lines as you would for other charted designs, then draw in two diagonal lines across the centre of the canvas. The diagonal lines must be drawn accurately as they are the point where the stitches turn. Start working in the centre, ensuring that you work an even number of stitches either side of the central line. This is of paramount importance if the design is to balance. When you come to the diagonal dividing line there may not be space to work the whole stitch, so smaller stitches need to be worked. It is best to plan the position of your pattern before stitching, as this will ensure that the design is pleasing to the eye.

Fig. 12 *The same pattern as Fig. 11 turned into a four-way design. Four-way patterns look far harder to do than they really are. Start in the centre and work one section at a time, working up to the drawn-in diagonals.*

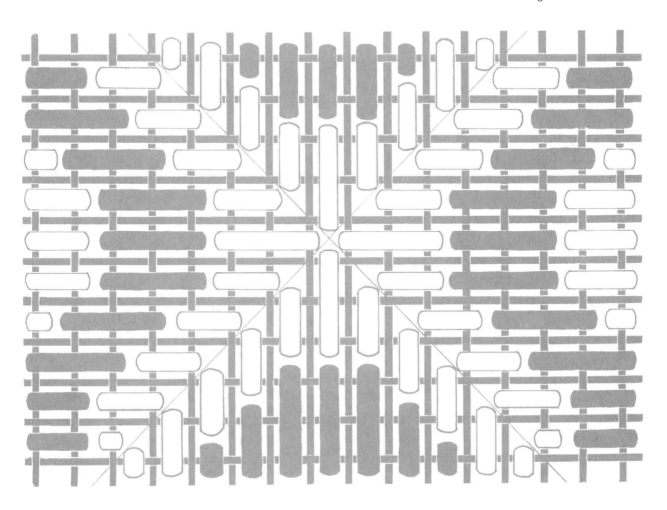

Long stitch designs are printed on to the canvas as an outline and straight stitches are then worked covering all the canvas. An illustration provided with the kit will show the correct positions of colours. As can be seen with this cat picture, sometimes the background is broken up with lines. This prevents the stitches from becoming too long and these lines will also be drawn on the canvas.

Fig. 13 *Starting off for long stitch canvas work. As long stitch does not hold the starting off thread at all, small running stitches must be made to secure the thread.*

Long stitch on canvas

This technique is becoming increasingly popular, due to the fact that it works up quickly. It is a very good way to introduce children to embroidery and there are many designs around that children will find appealing.

Start off in the area you are about to work, which should be the object most central, and in the foreground. Knot the thread at one end, work a few running stitches to secure it, then cut off the knot. Continue by bringing the needle up through the canvas in the hole you wish to commence working from. The thread must be started like this, because the long stitch does not hold the thread securely enough. To finish off, complete your last stitch so that the needle is through to the wrong side. Then weave the thread through the existing stitches about 1½ in (4 cm) in two different directions. Cut off any excess thread.

Working order for long stitch canvas work is the same as for printed kits. As most long stitch kits are pictorial designs, the background tends to be the sky and this should be worked last. There should be no canvas

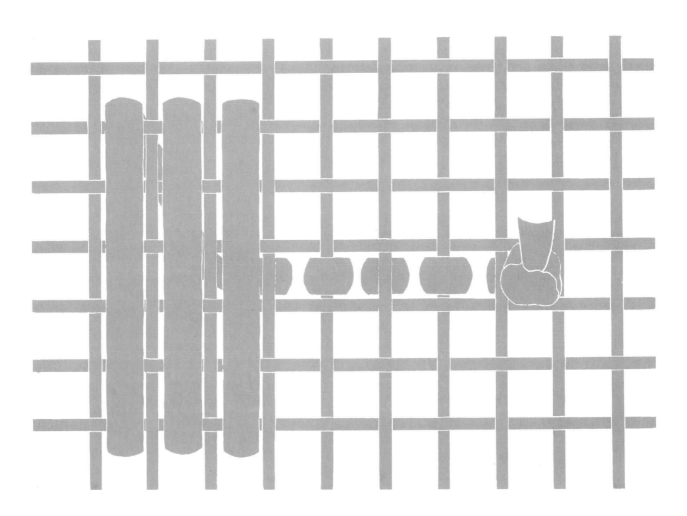

showing when the piece is finished, so when two colours border one another the stitches go in the same hole along the dividing line. Sometimes within the same colour there is a split drawn, and this should be treated in the same way. Any surface stitchery such as french knots should be worked last.

Tramé canvases

This technique originated when wool was of poorer quality than that we have today, so the traméd thread was used to pad out the stitches on the canvas. Today it is used to transfer a design on to canvas. This technique can be done only on double or Penelope canvas. A fine wool like crewel wool is laid on the canvas horizontally between the double threads to mark out the design. If there are detailed areas like hands and faces they will already have been worked in *petit point* and require no further work. The rest of the design and background is then worked in *gros point* over the threads of the double canvas. You match the thread colour to the tramé threads, then work over them using them as padding.

Fig. 14 *Tramé canvas work. This method can only be used on double canvas. The tramé threads go horizontally between the double threads, then tent stitch is worked over it.*

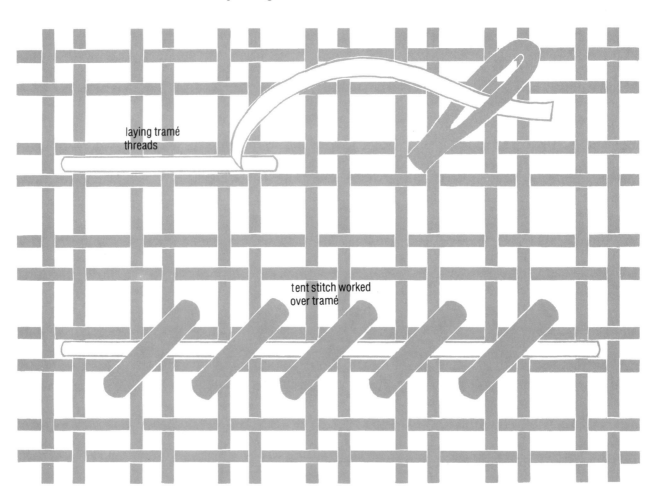

laying tramé threads

tent stitch worked over tramé

It is not necessary to tramé printed canvases or charted designs. It is also not always necessary to tramé the background on already traméd designs, but work a sample area first to see if there is a vast difference between the look of the design and the background area. If there is, you will have to tramé the background. Tramé is both thread- and time-consuming, so if it is not required, your piece will be completed more quickly.

WORKING THE BACKGROUND

The background shape should be drawn on to the canvas before you start to stitch, particularly if you require an unusual shape such as a chair seat. Rectangles or square shapes are easily drawn on at a later stage. The shape should be drawn with an HB or 2B pencil, making sure that it is square to the design. It is important, however, to trace on the outer perimeter of the background to prevent the common error of not completing the background rows correctly. It is very easy to misjudge this if you are calculating filling in the background by eye only. An accurately drawn background will ensure that making up is easier and more precise. The background can be worked in a different stitch from the design, and there are some suggestions on pages 57–62. By using a different stitch for the background you will be able to complete the area more quickly, unless you use cross stitch. Moreover, a contrasting stitch will give more emphasis to the design. When working the background, try to work whole rows. If this is not possible, however, the background can be worked in sections. When the background is being worked in this way do not finish the rows at the same point, but stagger the ends. This prevents the formation of a seam which would make your background look uneven. If you wish to use tent stitch for the background, choose continental (basketweave) tent stitch which will distort the canvas less, although you will need twice as much thread as you would for tent stitch.

It is not only the stitch you choose for working the background that can change the appearance of your work. Colour is also very important. If your kit does not come with background thread supplied, wait if possible until you have worked the design, so that you can see how the colours have worked together. It is essential to use a shade that contrasts with the colours in the design that border the background. If you choose a shade too close to these colours, you will find that the edges of the design merge with the background. The colour should also go with the décor of the room for which the piece is intended. Avoid using pure white as this will not only get dirty quickly but will also tend to glare. If you wish to use a light colour, choose a pastel shade which will complement your design. Black can also dramatically affect the

Tramé is a technique which developed when wool was of a poorer quality than that which we have today and the traméd thread was used to pad out the stitches on the canvas. Today it is used as another method of transferring a design onto canvas. It can only be done on double canvas, as the tramé thread, which is a fine wool such as crewel wool, goes horizontally between the double threads. Matching the colours to the tramé threads, work tent stitch over them, using the tramé as a padding. Tapestry wool is usually used to work the tent stitch.

colours in the design by making them look gaudy, so this too is best avoided, unless it is the effect you are looking for.

CANVAS WORK STITCHES

Most stitches that are in general use in canvas work are based on either tent stitch, long stitch or cross stitch. Stitches which originate from tent stitch or long stitch are quicker for filling in large areas. Those based on cross stitch take longer, as you need at least two stitches to cover the same area. I have included some stitches that are suitable for use as a background stitch, to complement the tent stitch design.

All the stitch diagrams are numbered so that the needle comes up through the canvas at the odd numbers and down at the even ones.

Canvas stitch sampler

1. Tent stitch worked in crewel wool
2. Tent stitch worked in tapestry wool
3. Tent stitch worked in Persian wool
4. Tent stitch worked in stranded cotton
5. Tent stitch worked in coton perlé
6. Tent stitch worked in soft cotton
7. Milanese stitch
8. Interlocking gobelin stitch
9. Continental (basketweave) tent stitch
10. Wrong side of continental (basketweave) tent stitch
11. Wrong side of tent stitch
12. Wrong side of half cross stitch
13. Cashmere stitch
14. Parisian stitch
15. Canvas shading using six different shades and tweeding to create softer shading
16. Moorish stitch
17. Hungarian variation

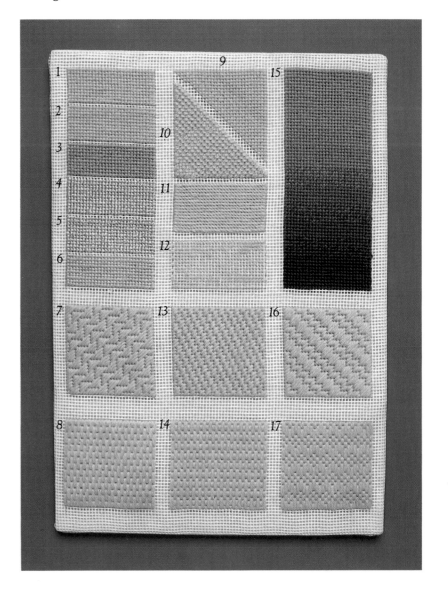

53

Tent stitch

Tent stitch is the most commonly used canvas stitch and is the one often referred to as tapestry stitch. It is a small diagonal stitch on the right side worked over one intersection. On the wrong side it creates a large diagonal stitch, which is referred to as a long stitch. This method of working uses more wool than half cross stitch and gives a firmer finish to your work. At the end of each row when you need to change direction to start the next row, you will have to do a small vertical stitch on the wrong side to give you the starting point of the next row. There are times when you cannot do a long stitch – for example, when you have areas of dots consisting of one stitch.

Get into the good habit of working with a long stitch on the back, even when you are not working a neat square, as shown in Fig. 15.

Fig. 15 *Tent stitch. This is the most frequently used stitch in canvas work. It is often called tapestry stitch because it resembles woven tapestry when worked on fine canvas.*

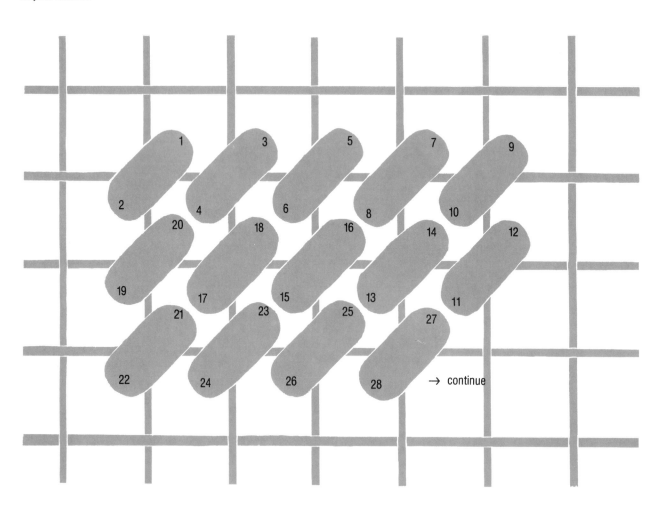

Fig. 16 *Working tent stitch in different directions. A better finish is achieved if a long stitch is created on the wrong side. This diagram will help when working tent stitch in various directions.*

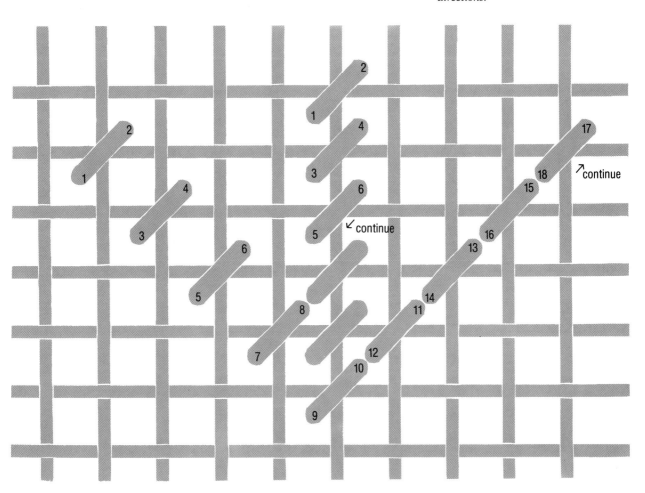

Continental (basketweave) tent stitch

This stitch is a little more complicated and needs fairly large areas to work within, so that you can get the rhythm of the stitch correct. If you are going to use tent stitch for your background it is preferable to use continental (basketweave), because although it looks like tent stitch on the front it gives a basketweave effect on the back which does not distort the canvas as much. However this stitch uses more thread than ordinary tent stitch. It is worked in diagonal rows across the canvas, starting in the top right corner as in Fig. 17. When you start it seems like an impossible pattern to follow, but once the penny drops you will wonder what all the fuss was about. A guide is that when the row comes from the top the bottom thread across the back should be going vertically and when you are doing the return journey the thread should lie horizontally.

Fig. 17 *Continental (basketweave) tent stitch. Although on the right side this stitch looks like tent stitch, on the wrong side it creates a basketweave effect – hence one of its names. The stitch is worked in diagonal rows.*

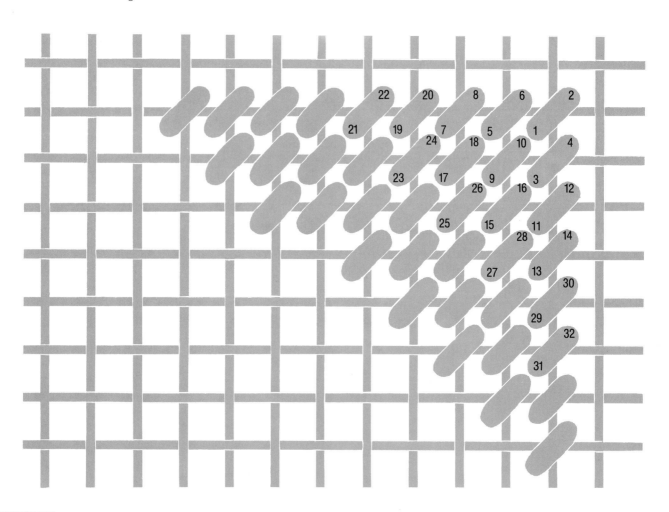

Milanese stitch

Milanese stitch gives a brocade or damask look and is effective for the background when the design has been worked in tent stitch. It can also be used for the design instead of tent stitch, but the working areas would need to be quite large for the stitch to look its best.

It is based on tent stitch and consists of a tent stitch and a series of progressively elongated stitches which together form a triangle. The rows are worked diagonally. One row points upwards, the other downwards, so that the triangles interlock. See Fig. 18.

Fig. 18 *Milanese stitch. This stitch is good to use for background or large open areas of design as it fills up more quickly than tent stitch.*

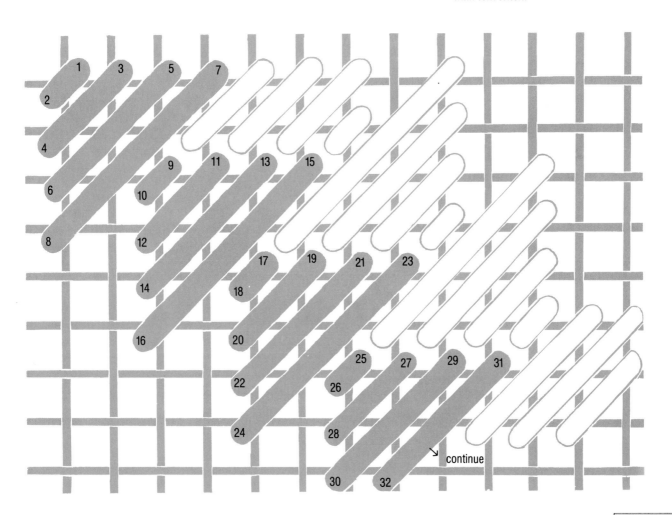

Cashmere stitch

This stitch is also based on tent stitch but it consists of a tent stitch, then two elongated stitches each over two threads, then another tent stitch. Together they form a rectangle. The last tent stitch is used as the first tent stitch of the next rectangle. Cashmere stitch is worked in diagonal rows which interlock with one another. It works well as a background stitch when the design has been worked in tent stitch. It can also be used to work the design but will only look good if the area is large enough to get a pattern repeat. See Fig. 19.

Fig. 19 *Cashmere stitch. This stitch is worked in diagonal rows and makes an effective background stitch.*

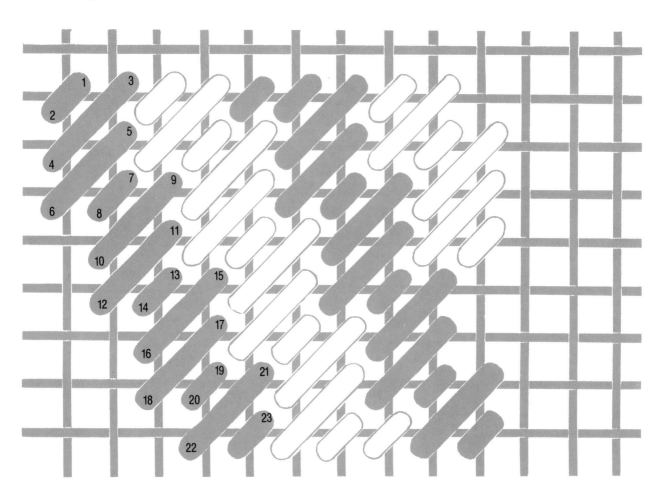

Moorish stitch

This stitch consists of blocks of five stitches, the longest in the middle, with two progressively smaller ones on either side. The smaller stitch forms the starting and finishing stitch of adjacent blocks. The blocks are worked diagonally. Around the blocks is a border of tent stitches worked over two threads which follow the outline of the blocks. This creates a stepped effect. Moorish stitch is really only suitable for background as it has a large pattern repeat – it can be used for the design if the area is large enough, especially on fine canvas. See Fig. 20.

Fig. 20 *Moorish stitch is a good background stitch as it covers large areas quickly. The bordering tent stitches could be worked in a contrasting shade to add dimension.*

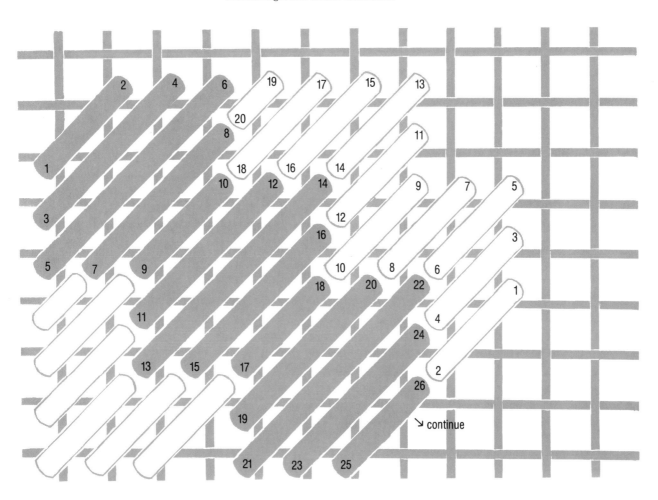

Interlocking Gobelin stitch

This is based on straight stitch and can be worked over any even number of threads. (The diagram and sample have been worked over four vertical threads.) Stitch one row of long stitches, leaving a gap of one hole to be filled in by the next row. Then work the next row coming back in the opposite direction, filling in the gaps and dropping the stitch down half a length to interlock with the first row. Keep the stitch in the second row over the same number of threads. See Fig. 21.

Fig. 21 *Interlocking Gobelin stitch.*

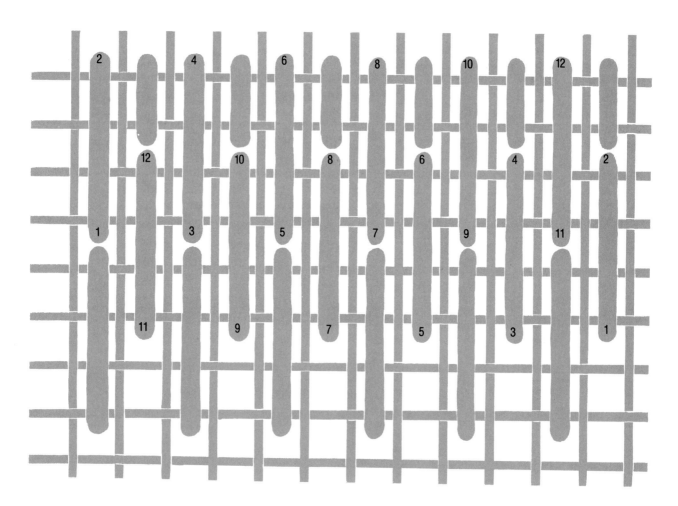

Parisian stitch

Another straight stitch which consists of rows of stitches worked alternately over four threads and two threads. The smaller stitch is dropped down one thread from the top of the larger stitch. The next row is worked in the same way, but the small stitch of the second row goes directly under the longer one of the first, so that the rows interlock. See Fig. 22.

Fig. 22 *Parisian stitch.*

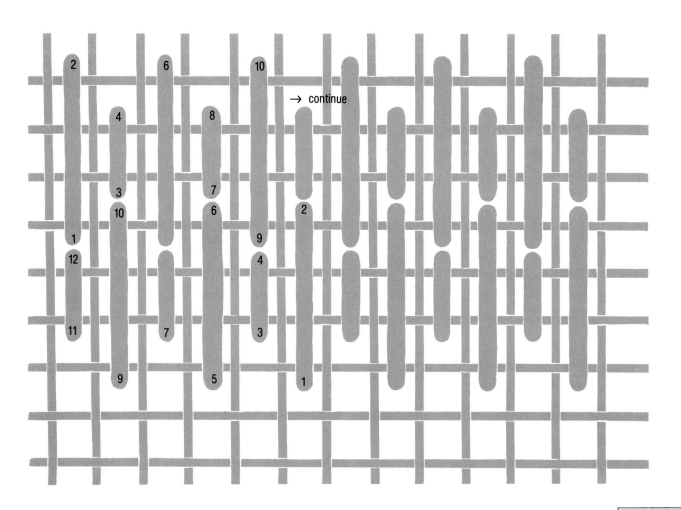

Hungarian variation

This is made up of stepped straight stitches. Working over four threads, three stitches up then three down form a repeating zigzag. The next row goes down, then up, forming a mirror image of the first row. This creates a converging zigzag in the gaps of which four straight stitches are worked over two threads making a little cross; the two stitches are above one another. See Fig. 23.

Fig. 23 *Hungarian variation.*

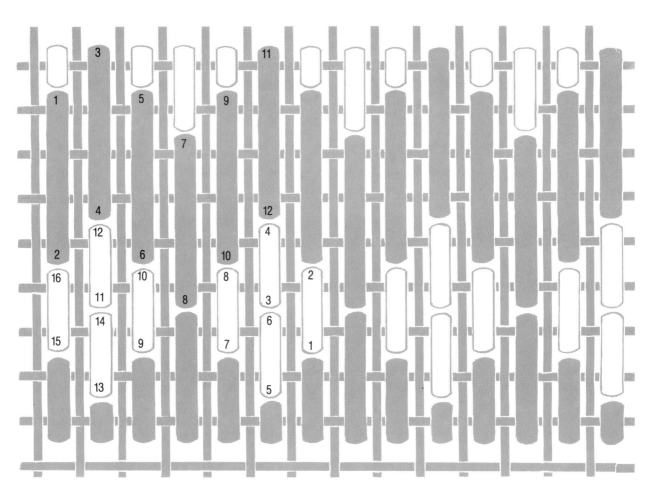

❧ 4 ❧

Cross Stitch

Cross stitch has a long history. The oldest known surviving piece dates from AD 700 and was found in a Coptic cemetery in Upper Egypt. Cross stitch has long been used on peasant costumes in Russia, the Middle East, parts of the Mediterranean and northern Europe. In the Middle East, where traditional clothes are still worn by many women, cross stitch embroidery continues to be very popular. The most ancient piece of English cross stitch can be seen on the Badge of the Knights Templar, on the Syon Cope in the Victoria & Albert Museum, London.

Cross stitch was used during the eighteenth and nineteenth centuries in western countries on samplers worked by young girls. This was part of their education, to teach them patience and good manners, in addition to needlework. Then in the 1920s a group of embroiderers, headed by Louisa Pesel, rediscovered traditional cross stitch designs. They set out to revive the technique as well as many other styles of embroidery.

Today a wide range of cross stitch designs are available, both traditional and contemporary, including famous buildings, cartoon characters and picturesque scenes. There are infinite variations on the sampler, but unfortunately very few kits seem to use peasant styles of design which are very attractive. Pattern books are available, however, from all over the world.

Printed cross stitch kits (opposite) come with a chart which has symbols to represent suggested colours. To make it easier to identify the colours when stitching, label each colour with the appropriate symbol. When stitching a printed design it is important to cover the printed crosses and not to count the threads of the fabric, which will usually be a closely woven one such as cotton sateen. The print will generally be permanent and so will not disappear with washing.

When using charted cross stitch kits (right) there will be no markings on the fabric. As with the printed kits there will be a chart included which will have symbols to represent colours. Each square on the chart is equal to one cross stitch on the fabric, and on some fabrics the cross will have to go over more than one thread.

TYPES OF CROSS STITCH KITS

Charted

The design is drafted on to squared paper and is either in colour or more often uses a symbol to represent each colour. The fabric can be aida or an evenweave fabric. There will be no markings on the fabric itself.

Printed

It is getting harder to find cross stitch patterns that are printed on to the fabric. Most will be charted, although a few companies produce designs in both forms. Printed designs will be arranged so that you stitch over the printed crosses. These kits generally use closely woven fabric, as it is impossible for the design to be printed accurately on an evenweave fabric. There will also be a drawing or chart to indicate the position of the colours.

STARTING AND FINISHING OFF

Follow the instructions in chapter 3 for starting and finishing off canvas work. Unlike canvas work, however, not all the fabric is going to be covered with embroidery, so the starting and finishing off must all be done under areas that are going to be stitched. For spot designs (small motifs surrounded only by fabric), start off as normal but leave a longer length of thread about 2 in (5 cm). When you have finished the motif, weave the ends in through the back of the stitches. This prevents ugly-looking bits of thread showing under unworked areas when mounted. The loop method can also be used if you have an even number of threads.

Do not weave too many threads under one area, however, as this will create an uneven finish, and always weave threads in two opposite directions to make sure that they are secure.

THE STITCHING

Cross stitch is basically two tent stitches passing over each other in opposite directions. (See Fig. 24.) The under stitch goes from the bottom right corner to the top left and the top stitch goes from the bottom left to the top right. The stitch must always go over the same number of threads across and up, so that it forms a square. Work each stitch individually, making sure that the top stitch always lies in the same direction, or the light will reflect differently off the stitches and give a rough appearance. For long rows in the same colour all the bottom stitches can be worked, going from left to right, then the top stitches added coming back.

Back stitch can also be used on cross stitch pieces, to outline areas and stitch in details. This should always be done after the cross stitches have been worked. The back stitch should be the same length as the cross stitch, so if the cross stitch is two threads square then the back stitch should be two threads long. (See Fig. 26.) Bring the needle up through the fabric two threads in front of where you wish the outlining to start, then go down through the fabric at the starting point. Next bring the needle up two threads in front and go back through the fabric in the same hole as the first stitch. Continue as above.

Fig. 24 *Cross stitch. All the top stitches must go in the same direction. It will create a rough effect if they do not.*

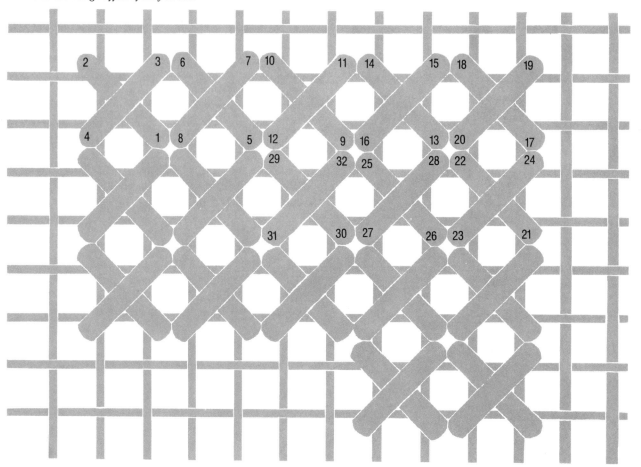

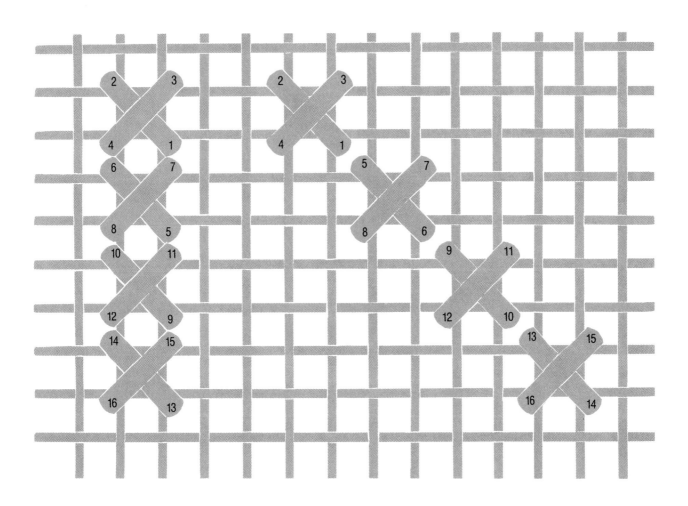

Fig. 25 *Cross stitch worked diagonally and vertically. Because the fabric is usually an open weave, it is important to have as little thread as possible travelling across the wrong side.*

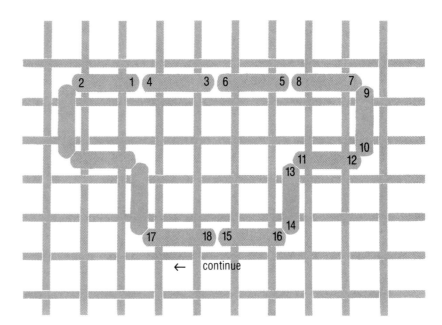

← continue

Fig. 26 *Back stitch worked on counted thread. Work from left to right. This stitch is used in cross stitch designs to outline and add definition.*

HINTS FOR CROSS STITCH

The crosses should lie smoothly over the intersections of the fabric without any twists in the threads. They should not split the threads of their neighbouring stitches.

When you are stitching do not pull the thread too hard, as this will create a large hole at the corner of the cross stitch. This is a particular danger with evenweave fabrics. The use of a frame will help with this problem, and will also make counting easier and more precise.

WORKING A CROSS STITCH DESIGN

Use the instructions in chapter 2 for following a chart. Always start a charted design in the centre, as this will ensure that your design fits on to the fabric. If there is no design in the centre, carefully count out from the centre to the nearest part of the design. It is important to remember that each square on the chart represents a stitch, so if the stitch covers two threads you must count two threads to the square. By counting carefully at the start you will reduce the amount of unpicking, although it must be said that even the most proficient embroiderer has to unpick sometimes. Unpicking is time-consuming, wastes thread and when dark colours are stitched on pale fabrics you may find that residue fibres leave a dirty-looking patch.

Whereas with canvas work no canvas should be visible through the stitching, with cross stitch the stitches do not cover the fabric as solidly, so you will get the fabric colour showing through. This is characteristic of cross stitch embroidery.

When the fabric is already printed with the crosses work from the centre outwards, using the same rules that apply to canvas work – that is, work the area that is in the foreground, for pictorial designs. If the design has printed outlines, keep all the stitching within those lines. When half stitches are printed next to an outline, make only half a stitch, and if a stitch is printed over an outline that separates two colours, work half stitches in a corresponding colour up to the outline. All outline and surface stitchery should be worked last. It is important that you cover the printed crosses accurately and keep them even so that they look as though they are worked on evenweave fabric. Using a frame will make this easier.

5

Crewel Work

Crewel work, or Jacobean work, as it is sometimes called, started in the seventeenth century and was popular till the early eighteenth century. It was fashionable to use it on soft furnishings such as coverlets and bed-hangings. These pieces were worked by both professional and amateur embroiderers. The designs were influenced by the eastern art and textiles that were being brought back via the trade routes. On the whole these were based on the tree of life, which was depicted as growing from hillocks. In these traditional panels little background fabric is to be seen, the spaces being filled with scrolling foliage and beasts. The most commonly used stitches were block shading, satin stitch, long-and-short shading (soft shading) and lattice-type fillings. These gave solid blocks of embroidery and colour interspersed with lacy areas.

There was a great resurgence in crewel embroidery during the early twentieth century, fostered by the Arts and Crafts Movement in which William Morris played an important role. Morris, with his daughter May, designed and worked many crewel panels. Some of these panels are available in kit form, although a few of the designs have been translated to canvas work instead.

The kits available today tend to be based on the Jacobean designs. The colours are usually less subdued, however, than the traditional dark blues, greens and browns that were originally used in those times.

TYPES OF CREWEL WORK KITS

Crewel work kits are worked on a solid stable fabric such as linen twill or cotton sateen. The design will probably be printed on the fabric as an outline, but it may be a transfer and in this case must be ironed on (see chapter 2). Crewel work is always stitched in fine wool, such as crewel or Persian. The kit will also contain an illustration, which usually has a letter and a number code to give the position of the colours and stitches.

STARTING AND FINISHING OFF

All starting and finishing off in crewel work must be done in areas of the design. To prevent shadows under the fabric, you should also not travel across the back of the work unless it is under sections that are going to be stitched.

To start off, thread your needle and put a knot in the thread at the opposite end. Take the needle through the fabric about 1 in (2.5 cm) away from your starting point, work a few stab stitches so that the thread is secure, then snip off the knot.

To finish off, bring the needle up approximately 1 in (2.5 cm) away from your last stitch, then work a few stab stitches and snip off the excess. When there are no unstitched areas left, the thread should be woven through the back of the last stitches in two different directions, and the excess thread cut off.

For starting and finishing off on outlines and areas such as stems, use the same principle but run the stab stitches along the printed line. When you come to the end of an outline it will be necessary to weave the thread through the last stitches. They must not cut across the back of the fabric on the outlines of such things as scrolls, as this will create shadow.

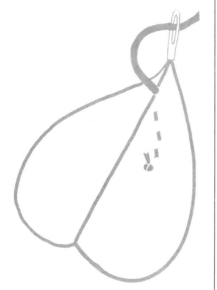

Fig. 27 *Starting off in a solid area. Work a few running stitches to anchor the thread before starting to stitch. The knot can be cut off once the thread is secure.*

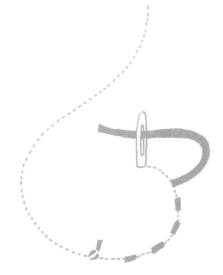

Fig. 28 *Starting off for an outline. The running stitch follows the traced line so that no thread is travelling across the wrong side under areas that will not be stitched, as this may cause shadows.*

HINTS FOR CREWEL WORK

Always work this type of embroidery on a frame. This will not only make it easier to work the various stitches but will prevent the fabric from puckering between stitched areas. A square frame is the most suitable for working large panels and a ring frame for small ones. If there is a great deal of heavy stitching on a panel, however, it could be marked when the rings are repositioned, so take care.

When laying down a basic lattice (see pages 75–77), keep to the same angle, working all lines in one direction first, then doing the ones in the opposite direction. The threads that are being laid down need to be taut but without pulling up the background fabric.

WORKING ORDER

When working a crewel work design you need to start in the central area, working objects that will be underneath further stitchery first. Working in this order means that you create depth with your stitching when areas overlap. Outlines should be worked last, as they are used to define areas.

When working a natural shape like a leaf, work from the tip down to the base – that is, opposite to the direction in which it grows. The stitches should be angled so that they point to the origin of growth. When working block shading and long-and-short shading, start stitching on the outer edge, going over any printed lines or split stitch if used. When leaf edges turn over, however, work a row of split stitch on the turned edge next to the last lot of stitching, then work this inner edge, first going over the split stitch. This will help bring the turnover forward.

Fig. 29 *Working order for crewel work; work areas that are underneath first, and stitch the vein last.*

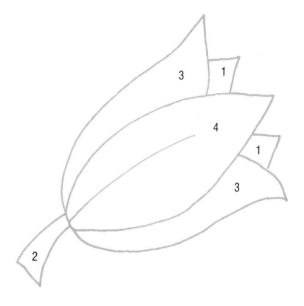

A crewel work panel showing various stitches including in the centre a long-and-short shaded flower and leaves. On the left there are two stylized flowers which have been worked using laid fillings. Some of the other stitches which have been used include French knots, stem stitch, buttonhole stitch and coral stitch.

CREWEL WORK STITCHES

Block shading

As the name indicates, the colours are worked in blocks to achieve a stylized shaded effect. The blocks are made up of rows of satin stitch, and after the first row, subsequent lines are stitched into the end of the previous row. This creates a dividing line without any fabric showing. Block shading can be worked in various forms: see Figs 30 and 31.

Fig. 30 *Block shading. This method of shading gives a stylized effect, as there is a definite break between shades.*

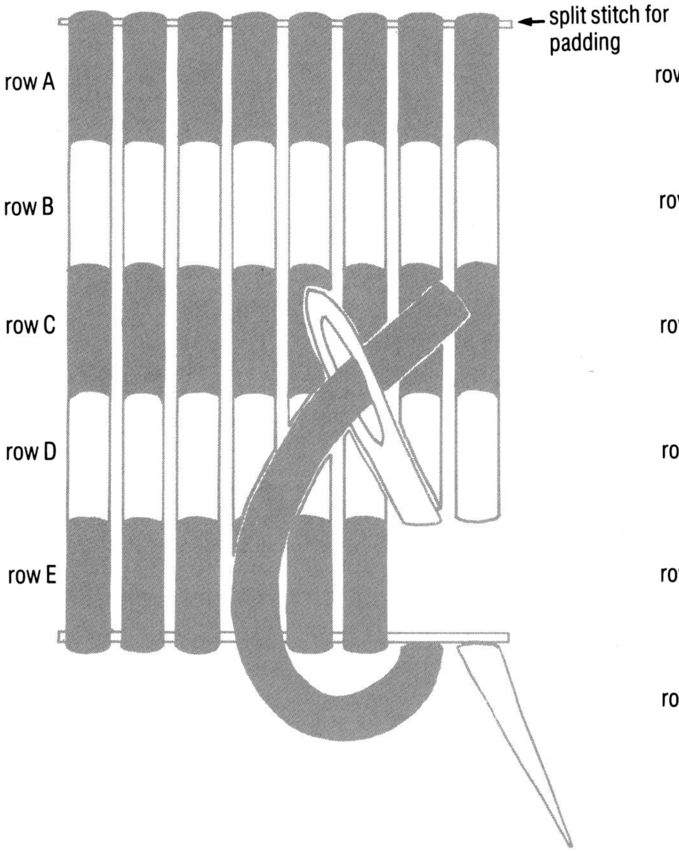

Fig. 31 *Block shading variation.*

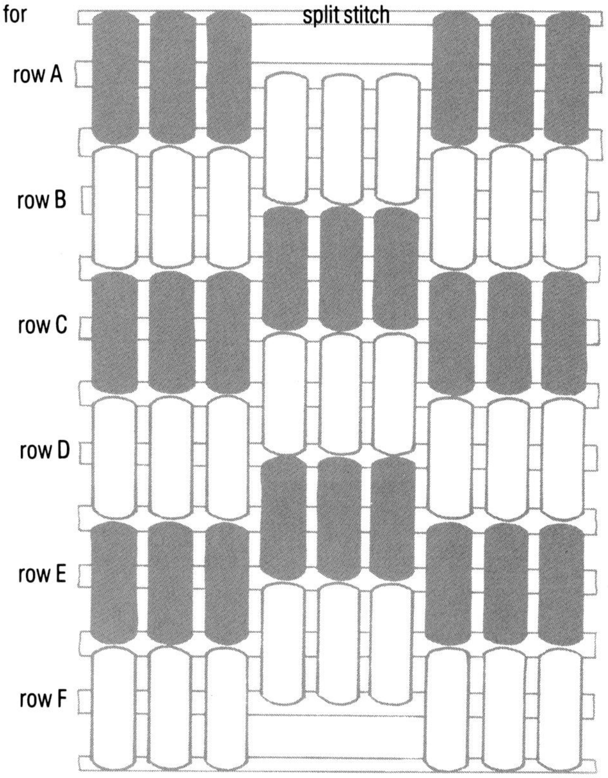

split stitch for
padding

row A

row B

row C

row D

row E

split stitch

row A

row B

row C

row D

row E

row F

Long-and-short shading

This type of shading gives a more naturalistic effect than block shading. There are two ways of shading which use long-and-short stitches, soft shading and tapestry shading. In soft shading, the stitches follow the shape of an area; the technique is used for objects like flowers and plants. Tapestry shading is chiefly used in ecclesiastical and heraldic work. Here long-and-short stitches are worked vertically, but to generate movement they are worked diagonally or spirally. Long-and-short shading can be worked in crewel wool, stranded cotton, stranded

Fig. 32 *Long-and-short shading.*

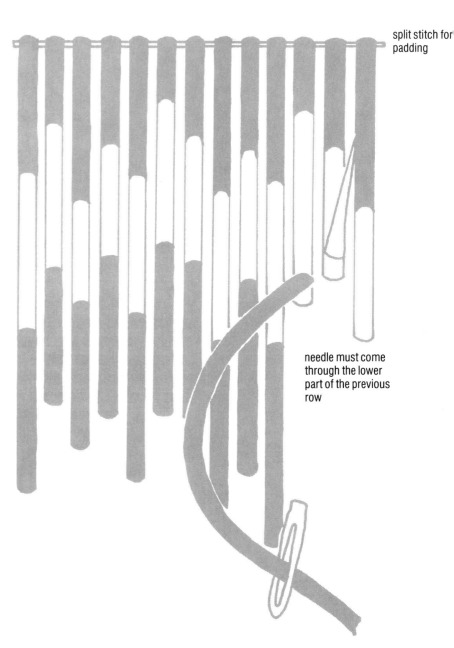

split stitch for padding

needle must come through the lower part of the previous row

silk and floss silk. It is best to work in a single thread or strand; although it will take longer to cover an area, the results are worth it. The stitches must lie flat and there should not be a hard line where the colours change over. It is a difficult technique to master and working a sample area is recommended. Start out by working a block using three or four shades and work in straight horizontal lines, before trying to fill in a particular shape.

Start off as for crewel work (see page 70), then bring the needle up from the wrong side approximately ⅜ in (1 cm) away from the edge. Take the needle down on the edge, making sure that you cover the printed outline. Copy this process for the next stitch but make the stitch a little shorter. Repeat these long-and-short stitches around the edge, keeping to the required angle if any. The stitches must be close enough together to cover the background fabric, but without looking cramped. The stitches should also not be of a uniform length, as this helps to create a more naturalistic effect. If the area to be worked is small and a ⅜ in (1 cm) stitch covers the shape, use satin stitch instead. This can be in one colour or in a variegated (shaded) thread. Long-and-short shading looks good only when long flowing stitches are used, as this results in a flat almost unstitched look. Working too many stitches in one area creates a rough effect.

The second row of stitches is worked by bringing the needle up through the end of the last row, then down through the fabric. Note that the stitches do not interlock with the previous row but come up through the end of the preceding row of stitches, splitting them. The stitches should be approximately ⅜ in (1 cm) in length. Continue working rows like this until you have completed the shape. The last row must come up through the previous row and then go down on the edge or into the vein of the leaf. For further information on silk shading see chapter 6.

Laid fillings

Laid or lattice fillings are used to fill in a shape. They consist of a basic lattice on to or into which other stitches are worked. French knots and cross stitches are the most commonly used.

As the area is not going to be worked solidly, you should start and finish off around the edge, which can be covered up with an outlining stitch. The filling stitches should also be started and finished in the outline.

When you are laying down the lattice, you need to use longer-than-normal lengths of thread, particularly for large areas. For making a basic lattice, see Figs 33 and 34. Note that the movement to the start of the next stitch is done around the outline and uses the minimum amount of thread.

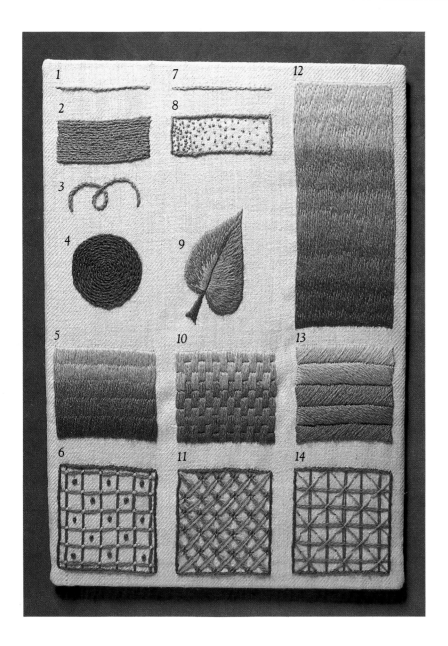

Crewel work stitch sampler

1. Stem stitch
2. Stem stitch worked in lines to form a solid area
3. Stem stitch worked in a corkscrew twist
4. Stem stitch worked in a continual spiral to form a solid circle
5. Blocking shading
6. Simple laid filling tied down with a small diagonal stitch and filled with French knots

7. Spilt stitch
8. Seeding
9. Long-and-short shading
10. Block shading (interlocking)
11. Diagonal laid filling
12. Long-and-short shading worked through six shades
13. Block shading (slanted)
14. Laid filling tied down with large cross stitches

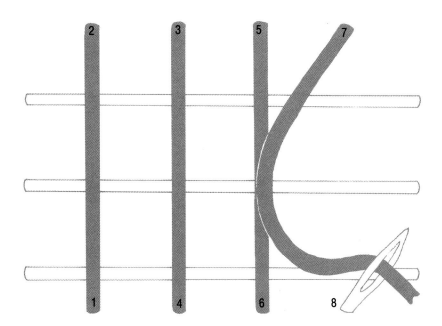

Fig. 33 *Laying down the threads for a basic lattice. The white lines were laid down first. The same method is used for working a diagonal lattice, and the variations on the lattice theme.*

Fig. 34 *The lattice can then be tied down with a stitch such as tent stitch.*

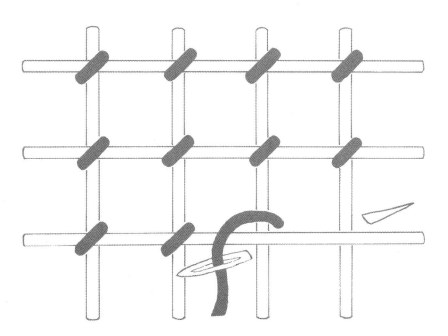

Fig. 35 *A diagonal lattice tied down with upright crosses, a variation on lattices. Interesting effects can be achieved by using different stitches and colours.*

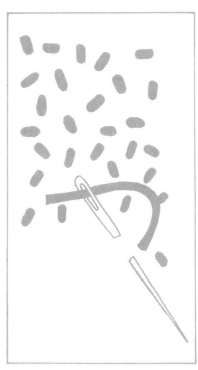

Fig. 36 *Seeding consists of small straight stitches, worked randomly. They can be worked closely or further apart to create a shaded effect.*

Seeding

Seeding is used to fill areas such as leaves and petals. It is made up of tiny straight stitches of the same length (approximately the width of the thread), which are randomly stitched. Start and finish off wherever possible in the outline, as with laid fillings. If there is no outline, start by working over the same place a couple of times to anchor the thread and form your first stitch. To finish off, weave through the back of previous stitches. See Fig. 36.

Stem stitch

A versatile stitch which can be used for outlining or can be worked in rows to fill a shape. Stem stitch is probably the oldest known stitch in the world. When worked, it resembles a fine cord on the right side and back stitch on the wrong. Following Fig. 37, begin by bringing the needle up through the fabric at the beginning of the line, then back down through the fabric about ¼ in (6 mm) away, still following the line. Then bring the needle up through the fabric halfway along the first stitch. Do not come through the stitch, but to one side of it. Once you have started, always come up on the same side. Then go down through the fabric, making sure that the stitches are the same length. The positioning of the stitches creates a cord effect. To go round curves and points, the stitches will have to be slightly smaller to compensate for the angle.

Fig. 37 *Stem stitch creates a small corded effect. It is used mainly for outlining areas but can also be used to fill in a solid shape.*

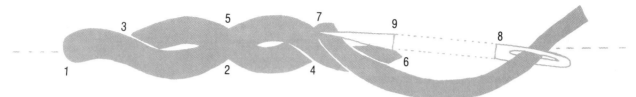

Split stitch

Split stitch is a very useful stitch which can be used as an outlining stitch or to give slight padding around the edge for long-and-short and satin stitches. It is also used to create a definite break or crease such as a vein in a leaf or a fold in a garment, over which long-and-short stitches are then worked.

Following Fig. 38, bring the needle up through the fabric at the start of the line, then take it down about ¼ in (6 mm) away, still following the line. Next bring the needle up through the fabric about halfway along the stitch, then take the needle down through the previous stitch, splitting it. The stitches will have to be smaller to compensate for the angle of curves.

Fig. 38 *Split stitch. Take the needle down through the previous stitch. Split stitch is mainly used as a padding stitch for satin stitch or long-and-short shading.*

❧ 6 ❧

Surface Stitchery and Silk Shading

Surface stitchery has a long and distinguished history in embroidery terms. It was traditionally worked in silk threads, but today these have largely been replaced by cotton.

The Chinese are reputed to have used silk as far back as 2000 years ago, but the oldest example outside China dates from AD 900 and is found on the maniple and stole of St Cuthbert, now in the Victoria & Albert Museum, London. These items, in common with other examples of church embroidery from that date, include a large amount of metal thread work. They are typical of the embroidery of the period from AD 900 to AD 1600 known as Opus Anglicanum, which reached its peak of perfection at the end of the thirteenth century.

Opus Anglicanum produced a high standard of design and technique. Professional workshops employing both men and women were set up. These craftspeople were highly skilled and well paid.

Surface stitchery is a very versatile type of embroidery and includes any stitching on a fabric that does not require counting. The stitches can be worked on any type of material, using different threads and stitches.

Silk shading is the embroidery equivalent of painting but uses a needle and thread to give a naturalistic effect. The kits that are available which use these techniques tend to be pictorial, depicting scenes and objects in a naturalistic way, although there are some stylized versions to be found.

A part-worked surface stitchery design being worked on a ring frame which shows the design as an outline that is then worked over with stitchery, starting with objects in the background such as the ear of wheat. The stitches used include long-and-short stitch, straight stitches with a combination of coton à broder and stranded cotton in the needle, padded satin stitch, laid filling over satin stitch, French knots and stem stitch.

TYPES OF KITS

In kits the design will either be printed on to the fabric or provided as a transfer. The background may be anything from silk, cotton or linen to a synthetic material. The threads are most likely to be stranded cotton, coton perlé or coton à broder, although some kits may contain silk threads.

STARTING AND FINISHING OFF

Surface stitchery is very similar to crewel work, so follow the instructions in chapter 5 for starting and finishing off.

HINTS FOR SURFACE STITCHERY

Always use a frame, a ring frame being suitable for small pieces and a square one for larger pieces. Do not travel from area to area, as the thread will show through on the right side and may pucker the fabric if it is pulled.

If the fabric is very fine and you do not want a transparent effect, use a backing fabric such as calico. The backing fabric must be pre-shrunk. To do this, simply wet the fabric then press it dry. Using a backing fabric also helps to prevent puckering. Do not use very thick threads on fine fabric, as this will cause distortion and make your work look untidy.

If you wish to use thick or textural threads, couch them down with a thread that is more compatible to the weave of the base fabric.

Do not use knots on the wrong side of your stitching, as this makes bumps on the right side. This is particularly important if the piece is to be used for table linen.

WORKING ORDER

Surface stitchery and silk shading are worked in the same way as crewel work, so follow the instructions in chapter 5.

To work long-and-short shading you need to stitch the areas underneath first. Start from the tip or upper edge of the shape and work down towards the base. Follow the shape of the area; for plants and flowers the stitches usually slant diagonally inwards towards the vein. After you have completed an area, to create depth split stitch can be worked along edges that are bordered by other objects. The split stitch is then worked over to create a slight raising of the surface. Another way to create depth is by using darker shades on the edges that are underneath and lighter ones on the edges that overlap. This exaggerated use of colour makes up for the lack of texture in the stitchery. The stitches must lie flat and give a smooth surface. This is why long-and-short shading always takes so long to master.

It is important to keep the angle consistent when stitching, although there are times when the stitches have to flow around the shape. These angles can be drawn on to the fabric, making it easier to keep the stitches going the right way. Draw the lines on the fabric using a 2H pencil. Make them straight, clear and about ¼ in (6 mm) apart, adjusting the angle where necessary.

On large areas where there may be several colour changes, you can draw on break lines to indicate when you wish to change shade. This could also be done on the illustration of the design provided with the kit. However, do not make these break lines too noticeable as there should not be a sharp division.

To work a linear stitch like stem stitch in a solid area, start by working the outline then work towards the centre in a continuous line. The stitch can also be worked in rows but each row must be finished off before starting the next row, or the last stitch will not hold.

STITCHES

I have included here some of the simplest and most popular stitches, but there are many more. If you find a stitch difficult, you can easily replace it with a stitch you can work.

Chain stitch

This can be worked either as a line or as a filling stitch. The chains should be regular in size, lie flat and have a rounded look. If the stitch is too loose it will look uneven; if it is too tight it will lose the chain shape. There are many variations on chain stitch, including zigzag, twisted and crested.

Following Fig. 39, bring the needle up through the fabric at the beginning of the line and take it down at the same point. Before you pull the thread fully though, bring the needle up through the fabric along the line you are following. Where the needle emerges dictates the size of the stitch. Put the needle through the loop and pull until the stitch lies flat. Check that the stitch lies correctly. For the next stitch, take the needle down into the hole where the thread is, then continue as before.

To finish off a row, bring the needle up through the last chain as if you were going to continue stitching, but take the thread over the last chain, then through to the wrong side to finish off.

The stitch can be whipped to give a corded look, either in the same thread or a contrasting one. To do this, bring the needle up through the fabric where the first stitch started, then, not passing through the fabric, slide the needle under each stitch, always going in the same

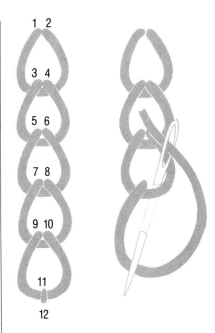

Fig. 39 *Chain stitch. The chains should look full and round wihout being too loose. There are many chain stitch variations.*

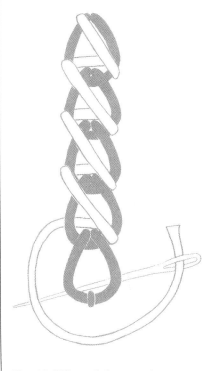

Fig. 40 *Whipped chain stitch.*

direction. To finish off, complete your last stitch then take the needle to the wrong side.

Satin stitch

This stitch is used to create a solid smooth area of colour. It can be padded slightly by using split stitch along an outline, which is then stitched over. For a more raised look, straight stitches can be worked in an area and then covered with satin stitch. For a very raised satin stitch, layers of straight stitches can be used. Each layer must fall in a different direction, and the last layer must lie in the opposite direction to the way the satin stitch will go. Satin stitch should never be longer than 1 in (2.5 cm), as it can easily be snagged especially on household items like cushions. If you need to cover a large area, either work long-and-short stitches or divide the area up and work satin stitch. Satin stitch looks smoothest when it is worked in a single thread.

Using Fig. 41, bring the needle up through the fabric on the outside of the outline, then take it down over the opposite edge at a point which gives a stitch of reasonable length. The stitch can be angled or taken straight across the shape, but once you have started, keep to the same angle. Then bring the needle up next to the previous stitch and continue as before. The satin stitch should look as neat on the back as it does on the front. To work around curves, you will need to have more stitches on the outer edge than the inner one. To do this make some smaller stitches that do not go across the whole area, interspersed with the full stitches.

Fig. 41 *Padded satin stitch. Padding satin stitch gives it a richer look.*

Fig. 42 *Satin stitch worked around a curve.*

padding worked in a different direction to satin stitch

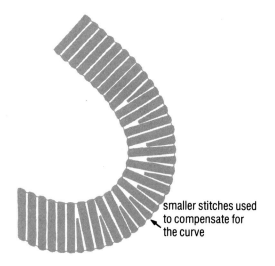

smaller stitches used to compensate for the curve

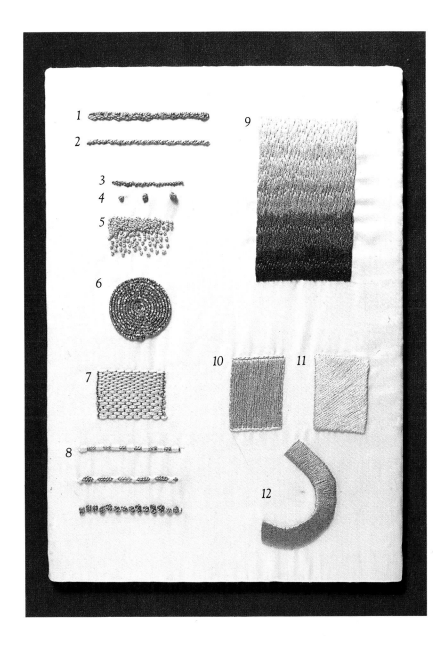

Surface stitchery and silk shading sampler

1. Chain stitch
2. Whipped chain stitch
3. French knots in a straight line
4. French knots in varying sizes using different number of threads in the needle
5. French knots worked like seeding
6. Couching in a spiral using Krenik facets thread
7. Couching in a solid area in straight lines, forming a pattern called bricking
8. Three variations of couching
9. Long-and-short shading using five shades
10. Padding for satin stitch
11. Satin stitch, worked over padding
12. Satin stitch worked round a curve

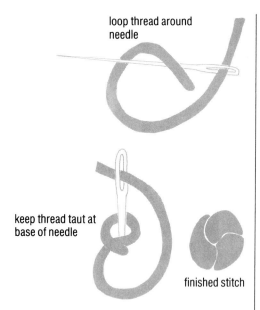

loop thread around needle

keep thread taut at base of needle

finished stitch

Fig. 43 *French knot. The secret to making a good French knot is to keep the thread that goes around the needle taut until the needle has gone through the fabric.*

French knots

These can be used to outline, for solid filling, or to break up a background. The size of the knot is determined by the thickness of the thread and not the number of times the thread is wrapped around the needle. The knots are easier to work on a frame, as keeping the thread taut is the secret of good French knots.

Following Fig. 43, bring the needle up through the fabric at the required spot. Point the needle away from the fabric and wrap the thread around the needle once. Then take the needle down through the fabric in almost the same hole. Do not pass the needle all the way through the fabric. Keeping the needle upright, pull the thread that is wrapped around the needle so that it becomes tight and lies against the fabric. Keeping the thread taut, draw the needle through, then go on to the next stitch.

Couching

This can be used for outlining or for filling in a solid area. Couching is very useful when you wish to use highly textured or very thick threads. Traditionally it was used for metal thread embroidery. A shaded effect can be created either by using a different shade of thread or by stitching closer or further apart. Different stitches can also be used to catch down the couched thread.

Following Fig. 44, lay the thread to be couched along the line to be followed, leaving an end of at least 1 in (2.5 cm). This end can be taken through to the wrong side later using a large tapestry needle. Bring a needle containing a finer thread up on one side of the thread to be couched. Then take the needle down through the fabric on the other side of the thread. These stitches can be angled or straight. Continue with these smaller stitches, keeping them no more than 3/8 in (1 cm) apart. When you have completed your line, take the end of the couched thread through to the wrong side and finish off the fine thread on the wrong side.

Stem stitch, split stitch and long-and-short shading, which are explained in chapter 5, are also used in surface stitchery kits.

Fig. 44 *Simple couching. Couching is a good way of filling in areas and stitching down textural threads.*

❧ 7 ❧

Making Your Own Kit

Embroidery is a huge and varied subject, and modern fabrics and threads are a wonderful medium in which to explore your own creativity.

After working a few embroidery kits you may wish to experiment and design your own piece. This need not be as daunting as it sounds. You can start by adapting a commercial kit, using different threads, different stitches or adding beads.

Although not all kits are suitable, most are open to some sort of adaptation. It is really a matter of having a go; you will find that some ideas work and others do not, but this is all part of the learning process. If you work samples of the stitches first, keep them for reference. By doing this you will build up a greater understanding of the technique and by discovering its limitations you will also learn to experiment within these restrictions.

In this chapter I have provided some ideas which I hope will inspire you to create a design of your own. Included are some simple ways to overcome the need to be able to draw which people often give as an excuse for not doing their own pieces. There are so many things around us that can inspire a piece of work. Remember that embroideries have been done using buildings, nature, computers, cars and even mathematical configurations as the original source material. Once you get an idea there should be no stopping you from creating some original pieces.

SOME POINTS TO REMEMBER

Experiments with embroidered articles that are to be used around the home are limited for practical reasons. Items that receive a lot of wear, such as rugs and upholstery, are not really suitable for adaptation. Although the Victorians were very keen on using beads and silk threads on such objects, unfortunately these materials will not stand the test of time, unlike wool. Rugs are best stitched in cross stitch as this wears well and causes little distortion.

Panels that are going to be hung on a wall are the ideal projects for experimentation.

Kits where the design is already on the fabric adapt well, but cross stitch kits cannot be used in this way.

If you wish to use different stitches on printed canvas panels, you should choose a design that is made up of good-sized blocks of colour or kits that are outline-printed. This is because you will not see the pattern of the stitch if the area is too small.

Charted designs are a little harder to go wild with, as you still need to count out the design. If you choose different stitches, however, or use beads that replace only one stitch, this should present no problem.

If you decide to use different stitches from those stated in the kit instructions, you may need extra thread. Most companies provide details of the shade number and the make of thread used.

IDEAS FOR EXPERIMENTS USING A KIT

The use of stitches is the main way of creating texture in embroidery. Some kits already use a variety of stitches, but you can still experiment with the finished effect by using different ones.

Canvas kits are readily open to exploitation of stitches. Most kits recommend tent stitch, but there are many other stitches that are more interesting. You may even find a stitch that resembles the object you wish to work. Bear in mind that cross stitch, by its very nature, cannot be changed through stitchery.

The use of thread is another way of creating texture, as it affects the way light is reflected. Using cotton thread in a wool panel, for example, instantly creates highlights. By experimenting with different combinations of threads, you will come up with some amazing effects.

Metallic threads can also be used for highlighting, or can be mixed in the needle with other types of thread. Do note that only certain types of metallic thread can be used in the needle. These tend to be lurex-based threads, so follow the manufacturer's instructions.

Beads are also very useful in embroidery. There are many different kinds, which can be used on all types of embroidery. They can be used randomly, to break up a surface, to replace a thread or to outline areas.

A detail of a sampler worked in cross stitch from a chart. The border which was on the chart has been omitted and details from the border have been drawn on to the card mount instead. This is just one example of how you can experiment with different ideas. You don't have to stick rigidly to the kit instructions.

Remember that you do not have to stitch everything on your fabric or chart. As long as the print will be covered and the design still looks balanced, it is up to you.

As well as leaving things out, you can add in simple details such as lettering – your name for example – or a border.

USING BEADS IN EMBROIDERY

Although beads tend to be associated with garments, they can be used on all types of embroidery. The Victorians were very keen on using glass beads on their Berlin woolwork. As long as they are sewn on securely, there is no reason why they should not be used on all sorts of items.

Sewing beads on canvas work

To sew on beads, use a polyester sewing thread, doubled in the needle then waxed a few times to strengthen it. You can use a beading needle or a number 10 crewel needle. The beads could be used to replace a certain shade, or can be stitched on afterwards. Start and finish off as for canvas work (see chapter 3), but leave lengths of up to 1¼ in (3 cm). To stitch a bead on, bring the needle up through the fabric as if you were going to do a tent stitch, then pick up a bead with the needle and take the needle through to the wrong side. Anchor the bead by working a tent stitch in the next hole before picking up the next bead and repeating.

Sewing beads on to fabric

Use the same thread and needles as above. Beads can be used to replace a thread, or they can be scattered where you think they would add to your embroidery or would make an interesting outline. If you require a solid area, they can be stitched on in rows or worked irregularly like seeding which is used in crewel work. Start and finish off as for seeding (see chapter 5).

When working straight rows for an area or an outline, bring the needle up through the fabric at the position you have chosen for your first bead. Take the needle through the bead, then down through the fabric. If the bead sits with the hole uppermost, bring the needle up through the fabric a little to the side of the last stitch and go back through the bead in the opposite direction. This will make it sit correctly. Continue to work the rest of the rows like this. For a seeded effect, stitch the beads down in the same manner but randomly. If the beads are going to be scattered more than 1 in (2.5 cm) apart, the thread will have to be started and finished off under each bead, to avoid having long trailing threads on the back of the work. All starting and finishing off must be done securely, as the beads can easily be snagged especially when stitched randomly. *Never* stitch beads on an article for a child.

DESIGNING AND ENLARGING

Simply mention design and drawing and most people protest, 'I can't draw.' There is a simple way of getting round the problem, however. You can use a postcard, photograph or some other illustration as the basis for your design. The object(s) in the design should be of a size and style that is not too complicated for the technique you wish to work. The illustration can also be used for the colour scheme and may give you ideas for stitches and threads.

Tracing a design

Trace off the design, copying all the lines you wish to transfer to the fabric. If the design starts to look complicated in line form then it is probably going to be difficult to translate into stitchery. Do not draw on shading lines or the direction of the stitches at this point, as they will add to the complicated look. When you have traced off the lines you may wish to enlarge your design, especially if you have used only a segment of the original illustration. If you are happy with your design as it is, go on to page 94.

Enlarging your design

There are two ways of enlarging your design. The quickest method is to use an enlarging photocopier. Many machines allow you to enlarge copies, usually specifying the percentage increase in size.

Two problems occur when enlarging, however. The copier can cause some distortion in the design. This is particularly obvious at the edges and creates problems if two or more sheets of paper make up the full design.

In addition, enlarging the design also enlarges the lines which you have drawn. After a certain number of enlargements it is sensible to retrace the design in its enlarged form, to reduce the size of the lines. If you then require further enlargement, simply repeat the process.

The other method is the use of a grid. Draw a grid over the design; for the average postcard a grid of ½ in (13 mm) squares should be adequate. Then on a separate sheet of paper measure out a square to the finished size of the design, and divide this up into the same number of squares as the original. If you wish to change the dimensions of the design by stretching it, this can be done by making the grid rectangular, but there should still be as many rectangles as squares on the original. Then, working a square at a time, draw the same lines as on the original. If

A step-by-step way of creating your own design for stitching.

1. Shows a photograph of part of the Houses of Parliament taken from Westminster Bridge.

2. A detail from the photograph traced and enlarged.

3. A 45° angle was drawn acoss the top corner and anything above that line was erased. The design was then re-traced and joined to the original to form an L-shape.

4. The final design which can be transferred onto fabric ready for stitching.

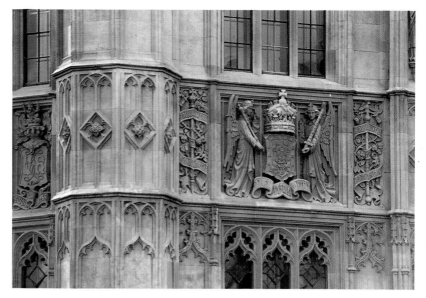

1

2

3

A detail of a printed canvas panel (left) which shows the use of beads. These beads were not included in the kit, but have been used instead of the wool provided. Using beads has made the peas look as if they are ready to burst out of their pods. By using beads or coton perlé you can create more depth in a design.

4

distorting the design by using rectangles, you will need to alter the angles. This method can also be used for reducing a design.

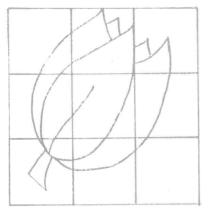

Fig. 45 *Enlarging using the grid method.*

TRANSFERRING A DESIGN

When you have got your design you will need to transfer it to the fabric. There are several methods that can be used depending on the chosen technique and fabric.

For cross stitch you will need a chart made from the design, and you may wish to create a chart for canvas work. For other techniques you can transfer the design directly on to the fabric.

Adapting a design for a chart

Start by using the method outlined above so that your design is the size you require. Remember that with charted designs, the embroidery will only come out the size of the chart if the fabric has the same gauge as the chart, and bear in mind that with evenweave fabrics you will be stitching over two threads.

Using a 2B pencil, trace the design on to graph paper or grid-printed tracing paper, which is also now available. The design must be drawn on in the required position, as its placement on the graph paper determines the way it will be when stitched. Now the design should be squared up, that is, the lines to be stitched matched to the squares of the graph paper. This is done by following the traced outline of the design but stepping the line by following the graph paper. Sometimes when you follow the traced line closely the stepped line does not look pleasing, so you may need to redraw some areas. When you are happy with the outline, draw in the stepped line with ink and rub out all the unwanted lines. You can either colour in the chart or use symbols to represent the colours. If you colour it in, remember to make the shade changeover lines stepped as well.

Prick and pounce

This method is used to transfer a design on to an opaque fabric and also when the design is detailed or repeated, like crewel work. It is a time-consuming method but accurate, and will give you good results. You will need several extra pieces of equipment:

A fine needle
A pricker   If you cannot get a pricker you can make one by pushing the eye end of a needle into a piece of cork, or taping it to the end of a pencil
Pounce   For light-coloured fabrics, pounce needs to be made of finely powdered charcoal and for dark ones of white chalk (or use talcum powder). Traditionally the white powder was made from cuttlefish. Pounce used to be sold ready-made, but it is no longer available. To create the same effect today it is necessary to grind your own charcoal or chalk. This can be done simply by enclosing it in a plastic bag and crushing it with a rolling pin until it is finely powdered. To create grey pounce, simply mix black and white pounce together
A pounce roll   This is used to apply the pounce. To make it, cut out a strip of felt or wool flannel, 6 in (15 cm) by 4 in (10 cm). Roll it up lengthwise to create a 4 in (10 cm) wide roll of fabric and oversew along the join
A fine paintbrush
A tube of watercolour paint or a 2H pencil
A soft pad   such as a blanket or towel
Tracing paper   Good-quality paper works better than a cheaper one

Trace the design on to the tracing paper, marking all the lines you wish to transfer. Place the tracing on top of the soft pad, which should be on a flat surface. Then using the pricker, pierce holes in the tracing paper

Here are the basic materials needed for four methods of transferring a design. Top left: pricking and pouncing. The design is drawn on to tracing paper then, using a needle, holes are made along all of the design lines. Fine powdered charcoal is then rubbed through onto the fabric.

Top right: tracing. This method can only be used on transparent fabrics like the canvas shown here.
Bottom left: charting. The design has been drawn onto graph paper then squared up, each square representing a stitch.

Bottom right: trace and tack. This method is used when no definite outline is required. Tack round the design using a contrasting colour then carefully remove the tissue paper. After the embroidery is completed remove the tacking threads.

along the traced lines, holding the pricker upright to stab holes vertically through the tracing paper. The holes must be close together, about 25 to the inch (10 per centimetre). You will soon get a rhythm going, but it is very important to be accurate. If the design is not very detailed the holes can be spaced out a little more, but always have a hole at an intersection or point. When you have finished, hold the tracing up to the light to check that you have done all the lines. The tracing with its holes is now known as a pricking. Press the fabric on which you intend to work the design and pin it out over a smooth firm surface. Frame it up, placing some books underneath to create a firm surface, if a square frame is to be used.

Place the pricking on the fabric in the required position and either pin or weight it down to prevent movement, as this will create blurred lines. Dip the pounce roll into the pounce and give it a gentle tap to remove any excess powder. Using small circular movements, rub over the pricking so that the pounce goes through all the holes and on to the fabric.

When you have done the whole design, remove the pins or weights and carefully lift off the pricking so that you do not disturb the pounce. If you find that you have missed an area or that the image is not very clear, the process can easily be repeated. First remove the pounce by flicking a clean cloth against the fabric, then start again. The good thing about prickings is that they can be used countless times.

To make the pounce lines permanent, either paint or draw in the lines. Water down the paint slightly so that it goes on to the fabric smoothly. Paint slightly inside the pounced line. Start painting from the bottom of the design and work upwards, covering the painted areas with tissue as you go, but do not lean on them or they will smudge.

When you have painted all the lines, allow the paint to dry. Then remove any excess pounce by flicking a cloth over the surface of the fabric.

On some fabrics, like satins, paint tends to bleed. In these instances use a 2H pencil instead to draw the line.

Tracing through the fabric

This method can be used only on transparent fabrics and canvas, when the embroidery is going to cover the lines.

The design should be on white paper and the lines must be strong enough to be seen through the fabric. If the lines are not strong enough, going over them with a black felt-tip pen will make them more visible.

Press the fabric and frame up if appropriate. Raise the design to the level of the fabric on the frame by placing it on something such as a pile of books, then rest the frame on top so that the drawing is in the required position. For fabric not framed up, pin the fabric over the drawing, making sure that it is on a smooth firm surface.

Trace through the lines, using a 2H pencil for fabrics and either a 2B pencil or oil paint thinned down with turpentine for canvas. It is important to choose a waterproof medium for canvas work, so never use ballpoint or felt-tip pens.

Trace and tack

This method is used when outlines are not going to be worked over but there are solid areas of stitchery, as in cross stitch. It allows you to change your mind, as the design is not permanently fixed to the fabric.

Trace the design on to tissue paper, then pin the tissue paper to the right side of the fabric in the position you require.

Using a pale-coloured sewing thread (dark colours will leave marks on the fabric), stitch along all the lines using a running stitch. Start and finish off securely, but do not leave any knots. The stitches can be longer on straight lines, but on curves and points smaller stitches will transfer the design more accurately.

When you have stitched all the lines, gently tear away the tissue, taking care not to undo the stitches. Running the needle along the line will break up any stubborn pieces. When you have worked the design these stitches can be removed.

❧ 8 ❧

Finishing and Making Up

As you will have spent many enjoyable hours on your embroidery, it is worth taking time and care over the finishing off of your piece. There are a few steps to follow before your embroidery can be made into something. These steps eliminate any distortion and ensure the work is clean.

By neglecting these processes you will not do justice to your stitching; even the most beautifully embroidered piece will look awful if badly made up. If you would rather leave it to the professionals, however, many embroidery shops offer a making up service.

Your embroidery can be made into an infinite variety of objects. In this chapter I have covered the construction of a few basic items.

STRETCHING
Stretching, or blocking, is the name given to the process which resets a piece of canvas work after stitching. This is so that the resins in the canvas set and keep the work square. All canvas work needs to be stretched, even if it has been worked on a frame.

Equipment needed
A wooden board at least 4 in (10 cm) larger than the piece of work. The corners should be right-angles and the board should not have been treated with any dyes that may be water-soluble

¼ in (6 mm) upholstery tacks

An old sheet or similar piece of cloth that covers the board

A tape measure or ruler

A set square

A hammer

1   Cover the board with the cloth, checking that there is nothing on the board or cloth that will mark the embroidery. Place the embroidery on top of that, right side uppermost. Snip into any selvedges to release the tension.

2   Place the selvedge along one edge of the board, so that it is flush with the edge and one corner.

3   Hammer in a row of tacks along these edges about 1 in (2.5 cm) apart, but do not hammer the tacks home as they have to be removed later. This gives you a right-angle with which to straighten the other two sides.

4   Tug and pull the work until it is square on the board, securing with tacks as you go.

This photograph shows a selection of completed articles including a framed sampler, bell pull, rug and four different cushions, showing an insert, piping and sewn on cord.

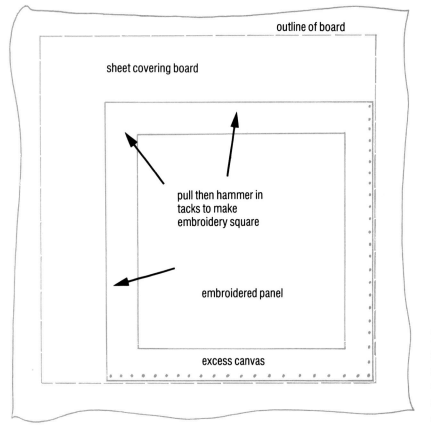

Fig. 46 Stretching. All canvas work must be stretched before it is made into anything. Stretching will re-square your work and the resins in the canvas will set in in shape once it has been wetted and allowed to dry.

5   When all four sides are tacked down, check that the panel measures the same in the middle across its width and length as along the edges. Also check that the corners are right-angles, making adjustments if necessary.

6   Dampen the embroidery with tepid water, dabbing it so that the whole piece including the excess canvas is wet. It should be visibly wet but not drenched. Do not rub your work when it is wet, as this will make the wool fluffy.

7   When your work is thoroughly dry, usually after a couple of days depending on the weather conditions, remove the tacks. Check all the measurements and angles; if the panel is still distorted it will be necessary to restretch it.

STEAMING

Steaming is used to remove minor wrinkles from crewel work and surface stitchery panels. It can also be used to freshen up a piece of wool embroidery.

1   Leave the embroidery in its frame, unless it is in a ring frame which covers only a part of the design. If you steam an embroidery in a ring frame you will be left with a mark.

2   Boil a kettle of water. Place the embroidery approximately 6 in (15 cm) away from the flow of steam, with the wrong side towards the kettle. Allow the steam to penetrate the fabric but do not allow it to become wet, as this will cause water marks.

3   When the panel has been steamed, allow it to cool and dry off but keep the frame taut. When the piece is dry remove it from the frame, unless there are still wrinkles, in which case re-steam. Sometimes the wrinkles are too stubborn to remove. The only permanent way to deal with this problem is to mount the piece over card, or to accept that a softer piece of work such as a cushion will contain wrinkles. If your work looks a little flattened after working or after a period of usage, it can be revived by steaming. Put the right side of the embroidery again about 6 in (15 cm) away from the steam but leave for a shorter period, not allowing it to get wet.

PRESSING

For surface stitchery, silk shading and cross stitch pieces it may be necessary to press the piece after working, especially if it is not going to be mounted.

1   Put the iron on the correct setting for the fabric you are using.

2   Lay a towel or something similar on a flat surface such as an ironing board. Place the embroidery face down on the towel.

3   Press the back of the fabric, being careful not to pull the embroidery out of shape.

CLEANING

If your embroidery is grubby from stitching it must be cleaned before it is made up. It is important not to iron the embroidery when it is dirty, or the marks will become permanent. Before cleaning, check the colour-fastness of dark threads and fabrics. Although most are colour-fast, it is advisable to test. To do this, take samples of each colour in the panel, dampen them, place them between two sheets of white paper or white cotton fabric, then iron over them till dry. If there is any loose dye it will show on the fabric or paper, and there is a strong chance that it will bleed during washing. In such a case, rather than submerging the embroidery in water, use a dry-cleaning agent. For pieces that are colour-fast and worked in cotton thread on cotton or cotton-mix fabric, the following method can be used. Using tepid water and a handwashing detergent (or a pre-soaking agent for stubborn stains), completely dissolve the detergent. Follow the manufacturer's instructions for quantities. The ideal vessel for soaking your embroidery is a bath or basin where it can lie flat. Immerse it in the water and leave to soak. If the stain does not look as if it is going, agitate the embroidery a little, but be careful not to scrub at the stitching. An old remedy for ring marks from the frame is to rub dry white bread into the affected area, this must be done on dry cloth. Wool embroidery rarely needs cleaning; dust can be removed by flicking a clean duster over mounted pieces or by plumping up cushions.

To clean canvas and wool embroidery, like crewel, the panel must be pinned out as for stretching (see pages 99–100), so that the piece does not become distorted. Dip a clean cloth into a weak solution of handwash detergent and wring it out so that it is only damp, then dab it over the surface, rinsing out the cloth frequently. Do not rub vigorously as you will make the surface fluffy. Allow the piece to dry before removing it from the board.

Embroidery on or in silk should be cleaned professionally. Some dry-cleaners or embroidery shops may offer this service. Check the suitability of the item for cleaning with your dry-cleaner. To reduce the amount of cleaning required, follow these simple tips:

●   To keep your embroidery clean, spray it before use with a fabric protection spray, several times.

●   Keep it out of direct sunlight, as this will accelerate the breakdown of the fibres as well as fading the colours.

- Dampness is also a great enemy of textiles, so keep them away from places that are damp or have great variations in temperature or humidity.

MOUNTING YOUR EMBROIDERY

There are two methods of mounting your embroidery on a backing ready for framing. The most commonly used method is lacing, but there is another method which uses herringbone stitch. Lacing is really suitable only for small panels, whereas herringbone can be used for all sizes, but particularly for canvas panels.

It is important to mount your embroidery on a good stable cardboard or hardboard that will keep your work square for years to come. When choosing a frame for your finished piece, take into consideration the depth of your panel when mounted, as well as any additional mounts and glass. Many modern picture frames are only suitable for thin pieces such as photographs and if not chosen carefully may give a disappointing result.

Like many aspects of embroidery, the use of glass on an embroidered piece is much debated. Its main advantage is that it prevents the embroidery from getting dirty and keeps it out of the way of investigating fingers. The drawback with glass is that it can flatten stitchery, although this is easily remedied by using a card mount to give depth to the frame. To make it match the piece, the mount could be covered with fabric. Non-reflective glass can also make an embroidery lose its life and texture.

The herringbone method

You will need the following materials:

Card or ¼ in (6 mm) hardboard cut to the required size You may need to use two thicknesses of card glued together
A curved needle
Calico
Glue, preferably rubber-based
Backing fabric such as cotton sateen
Pins
Button thread

1   Cut the calico so that it is 2 in (5 cm) larger than the board.
2   Cover the card with the calico, cutting into the corners to lessen the bulk. Glue the calico to the board but take the glue to only about 1 in (2.5 cm) from the edge of the card. This makes it easier

when herringbone stitching around the edge. (See Fig. 47.)

Fig. 47 *Board prepared for mounting. Keep the glue from the perimeter of the board as this is where the herringbone stitches will go.*

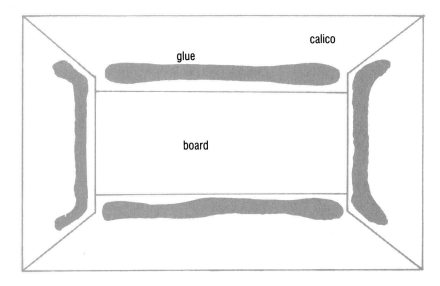

3   Place the embroidery on the card so that the covered part of the card backs on to the wrong side of the embroidery.
4   Start by pinning the corners of the panel to the corners of the board. Then push the pins about half their length into the side of the board all the way around, approximately 1 in (2.5 cm) apart. When pinning, check that you have kept to the straight of the grain, as this will ensure that the embroidery looks level when finished and that there are no wrinkles.

Fig. 48 *Embroidery pinned into position, with one side herringbone stitched back.*

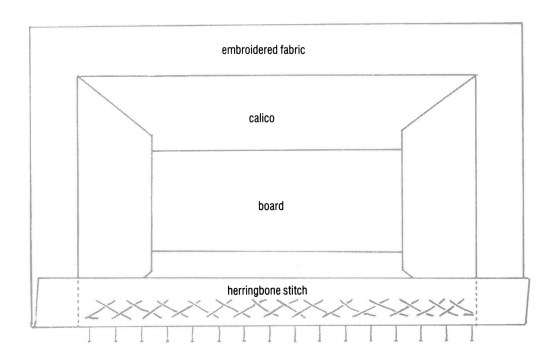

Fig. 49 *Herringbone stitch. For mounting, a curved needle will have to be used. Herringbone is a very useful stitch to know, as it can also be used decoratively in surface stitchery panels.*

5 Place the embroidery face down on a clean cloth.

6 Pull the excess fabric over the back so that it can be held taut by your non-sewing hand. Then, using a curved needle with double thread, herringbone stitch the excess fabric to the calico about ¼ in (6 mm) from the edge of the board. The herringbone stitches should be no longer than ¾ in (2 cm) and ½ in (13 mm) high.

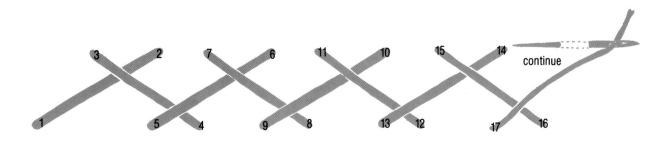

7 When you get to a corner, stitch to within ¼ in (6 mm) of it and secure the stitch a couple of times. Pleat the fabric so that there is as little bulk as possible at the corners and none protrudes towards the front edges. Do not cut the fabric to achieve this, however. Continue the process around the panel.

Fig. 50 *Pleat the fabric at the corners to reduce bulk. Do not cut into the corners especially with canvas as it may start to fray.*

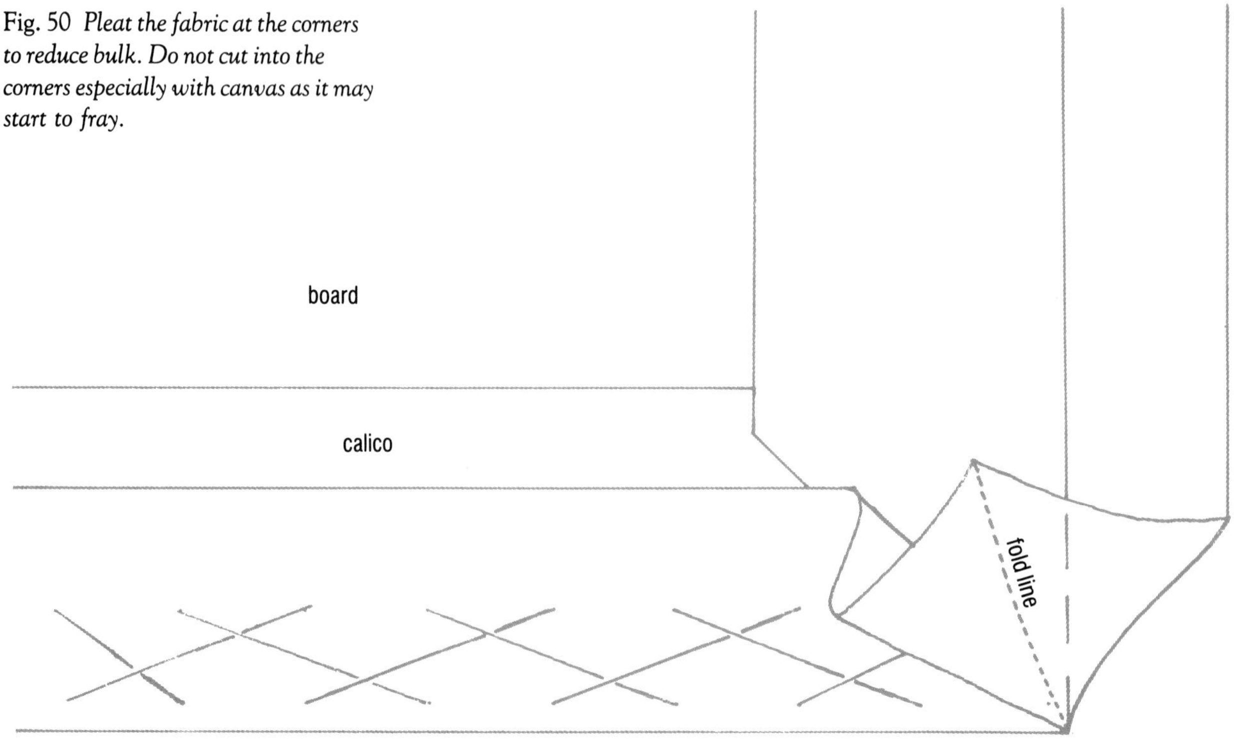

board

calico

fold line

8 The panel could now be framed or a backing sewn on to give a neater finish. To achieve the latter, cut the backing so that it is ¾ in (2 cm) larger than the board. Turn under the excess and pin it to the back of the panel so that you cover the herringbone stitches. Then slip stitch the backing on, using a curved needle and single button thread.

Your panel is now ready for framing.

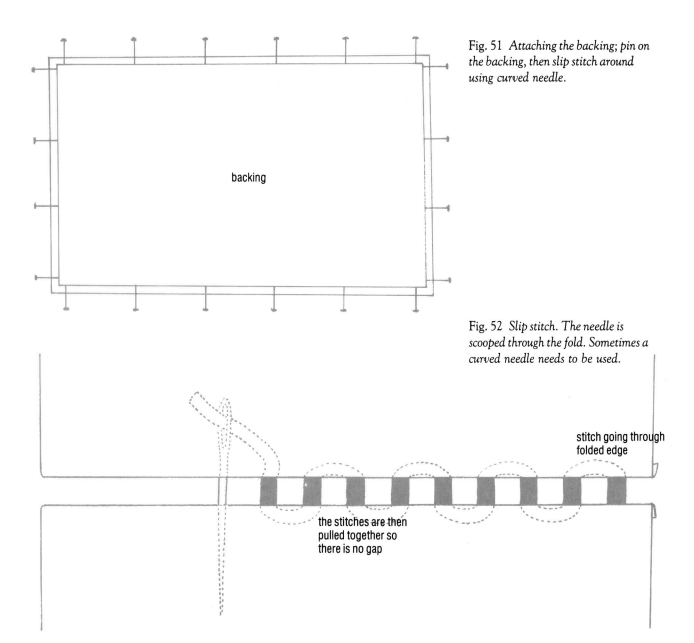

Fig. 51 *Attaching the backing; pin on the backing, then slip stitch around using curved needle.*

backing

Fig. 52 *Slip stitch. The needle is scooped through the fold. Sometimes a curved needle needs to be used.*

stitch going through folded edge

the stitches are then pulled together so there is no gap

The lacing method

1 Cut a piece of board to the required size. This board may need to be covered to prevent any colour coming through. If you need to cover the board, follow step 2 of the herringbone method, pages 104–5.

2 Finish off the raw edges of the fabric to be mounted with a machine zigzag or a single hem.

3 Follow steps 3 and 4 on page 105.

4 When the embroidery is pinned out, turn the work over. Take a length of thread sufficient to lace the opposite edges together and anchor it securely on one edge. Then stitch through the opposite

Fig. 53 *Mounting using the lacing method. This is really only suitable for small panels as it does not hold the panel as tightly as the herringbone method.*

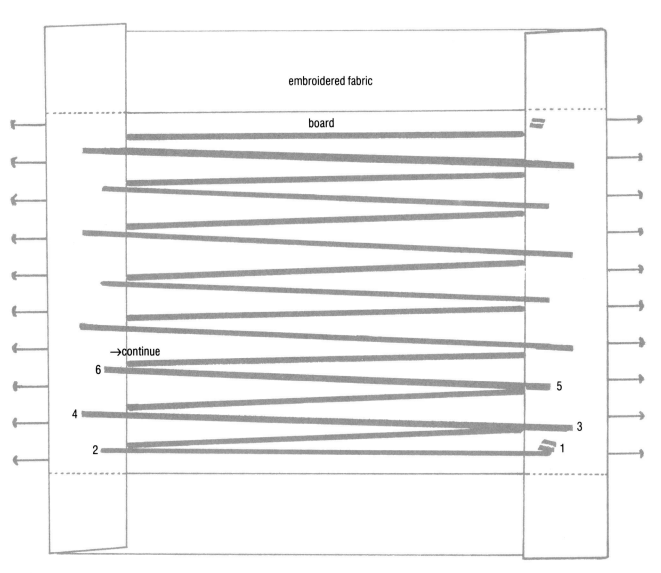

edge, pulling the thread so that it holds the embroidery in position. Stagger the stitches so that they do not pull the same row of threads. Continue until the opposite edges are secure. It is very important to keep the lacing taut, or the embroidery will not stay in position.

5 Do the same with the other two edges, folding in the corners slightly so that they do not show on the right side. Then remove the pins.

6 If a backing is required, follow step 8, page 107.

Fig. 54 *Lacing the other two sides to complete the process.*

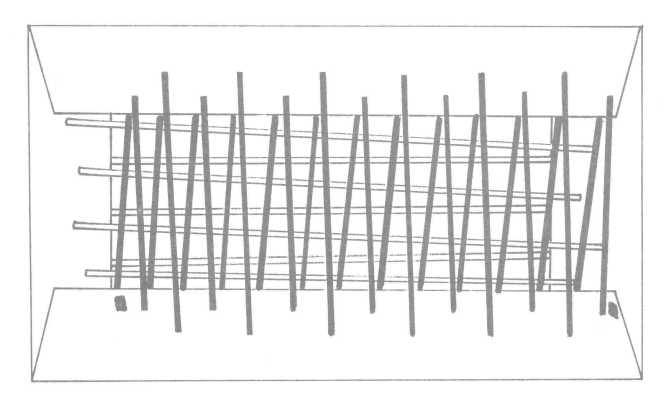

MAKING CUSHIONS

This section on making cushions is arranged so that you can mix and match the instructions. You could, for example, have an applied inset cushion with a frilled edge by using both sets of instructions. Do remember, however, to read carefully through all the instructions before starting.

Basic cushion with stitched-on cord

You will need the following materials:

Backing fabric of your choice   2¼ in (6 cm) larger than the finished cushion size

A length of decorative furnishing cord   about 2¼ in (6 cm) longer than the perimeter of the finished cushion

A curved needle

A sewing machine

For a basic cushion without trimming, omit the furnishing cord.

1   Prepare the piece of embroidery for making up (see pages 99–102).
2   Tack the backing fabric on to the embroidery with the right sides together.

Fig. 55 *Machine around the cushion leaving the lower edge open, apart from a small amount at the corners.*

wrong side of
embroidery

lower edge left
unstitched

seam allowance

3   Machine around the cushion, leaving the bottom edge open except for a 1 in (2.5 cm) line of stitching around the corners. For canvas work cushions, to make sure that no canvas is showing around the edges when the work is turned the right way out, swing the needle over to the left or use the zipper or piping foot.

4   Before you turn the cushion out, trim down the corners and excess fabric to about ½ in (13 mm), except at the opening where you need to trim down to ¾ in (2 cm).

corners
clipped

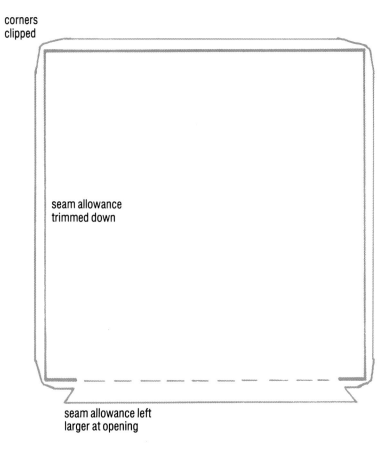

seam allowance
trimmed down

seam allowance left
larger at opening

Fig. 56 *Trim down the excess seam allowance, clipping the corners so that when it is turned through you will get a good shape.*

5   Turn the cushion right side out. Using a large needle, carefully lever out the corners, but do not pull too much or the corners will fray.

6   Insert the cushion pad, which ideally should be ½ in (13 mm) larger than the finished size, so that the cushion looks plump and will show off your embroidery to best effect. Make sure that the pad goes into the corners.

7   Pin the opening together, then slip stitch the opening using a double sewing thread. Leave a small gap, which can be used to hide the ends of the cord if used.

If you do not wish to add a cord, your cushion is now complete. To attach a cord:

1. Finish off one end of the cord by wrapping thread tightly around it several times, and fasten the thread off by sewing through the cord.
2. Push the end of the cord into the gap along the bottom edge. Stitch on the cord using a curved needle and double sewing thread. Sew through the edge of the cushion, using the seam as a guide, then catching the cord. As you are sewing, twist the cord, as it may start to unravel. At the corners sew through the cord several times. This is where it will bear the brunt of the wear and tear.
3. When you have sewn on all the cord apart from about 1½ in (4 cm), finish off the ends of the cord as before and cut off the excess. Push the end of the cord into the gap, then stitch on the remaining 1½ in (4 cm). Stitch through the cord so that the join is almost invisible; this may take a little practice.

Inset cushion

There are two ways of making inset cushions; either method is suitable for the types of embroidery described in the book.

You will need the same materials as for the basic cushion with no trimming, but double the amount of backing fabric.

Applied method

1. First prepare the piece of embroidery for making up.
2. For canvas work, trim down the excess canvas to 1 in (2.5 cm), then herringbone stitch this on to the back of the embroidery, mitring the corners so that no canvas shows on the front. The herringbone stitches should not come through to the right side but go through the back of the canvas work stitches. For other types of embroidery, cut a piece of interlining the size of the finished inset, then trim down the excess fabric on the embroidered panel to 1 in (2.5 cm). Place the interlining in the required position on the wrong side of the panel and herringbone stitch back as for canvas work, but only going through the interlining.
3. Cut two pieces of fabric 1½ in (4 cm) larger than the size of the finished cushion. Find the centre on one of these and also on the inset. Match up the two centres and pin the inset on to the backing, making sure that it is on the straight of the grain and that the inset is flat.
4. Now slip stitch the inset to the backing using a curved needle and double sewing thread, keeping the stitches small and neat so that they do not show. A cord could be stitched around the join, by stitching through the twist in the cord then through the fabric. To

join, finish off the two ends, poke them under the inset and then stitch the join together to make it almost invisible.

5 Make up as for the basic cushion.

Fig. 57 *Herringbone stitching back the seam allowance on an inset cushion.*

Fig. 58 *Stitching the inset to the backing fabric.*

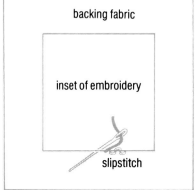

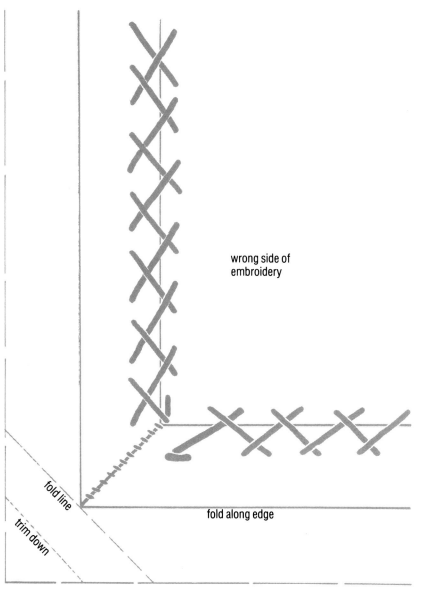

Strip method

1 First prepare the piece of embroidery for making up.

2 Cut four strips of fabric out of the backing fabric. The width and length of these strips, plus the dimensions of the inset, will make up the finished size of the cushion. Remember to add seam allowances.

3 Trim the excess fabric from the embroidery so that it is 1 in (2.5 cm) larger all round than the finished inset.

4 Pin, tack, then machine the fabric on to the edges of the inset.

5 The corners can be stitched two ways: either straight across the strips of fabric or angled. This is done by folding and pressing one edge over at a 45° angle, then topstitching on one side of the seam. Trim any excess fabric from behind. With the right sides together, mark a 45° angle at the corners and machine together, then trim the seam to ¼ in (6 mm).

6 Finish off as for a basic cushion.

Piped edging

You will need the following materials:

Extra backing fabric sufficient to make the cross-way strips
Piping cord long enough for the perimeter of the cushion plus 2¼ in (6 cm)

Most types of fabric are suitable for making the strips, but they must be cut on the bias/true cross. This helps to prevent puckering when the cord goes around the corners.

1 Cut strips on the true cross so that they are wide enough to fold around the piping cord with ½ in (13 mm) seam allowance either side. Piping cord comes in various gauges, so choose one that will look balanced around the edge of your cushion. Cut enough strips of fabric to go around the cushion, with a few extra inches for joining the strips together. Join the strips together (see Fig. 59), checking that the joins lie in the same direction and with napped fabrics that the grain is going in the same direction throughout.

2 Fold the cross-way strip over the piping, then tack close to the piping so that it is encased.

3 Tack the piping on to the edge of the cushion so that the final join will be in the centre of the bottom edge. On canvas work panels make sure that when the piping is turned back no canvas is showing. When you come to the corners they should be pointed rather than looking squashed and rounded. Allow enough piping to turn the corners, snipping into the cross-way strip if necessary.

4 To join the piping together, cut off the excess piping leaving a 1 in

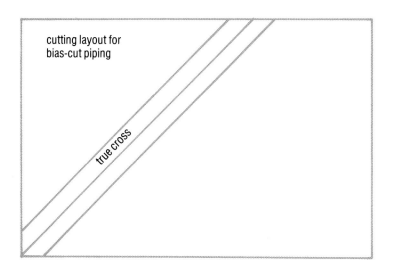

cutting layout for
bias-cut piping

true cross

Fig. 59 *Making bias binding for covering piping cord. The binding must be cut on the cross-way to prevent too much puckering around the corners. If several joins are required make sure that they all go in the same direction.*

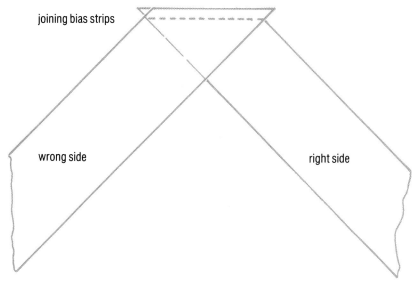

joining bias strips

wrong side

right side

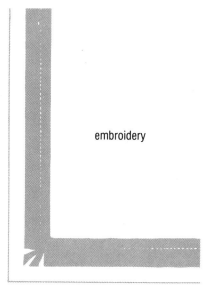

embroidery

(2.5 cm) overlap. Undo the tacking about 1 in (2.5 cm) either side of the join. Open up the cross-way strips so that the cord is exposed, then overlap the strips. Fold back the excess fabric on the cross-way strip so that it duplicates the angle of the other joints. Slip stitch the two edges together, then trim the excess fabric down to ¼ in (6 mm). Now finish off the ends of the cords (see page 112, step 1) so that when the extra is cut off they do not overlap. Cut off the excess. Stitch the ends together to make one continuous length.

5   Next, fold the now-joined cross-way strip back over the piping and tack down. Finish off as for a basic cushion.

Fig. 60 *Attaching the piping to the edge of the embroidery. Clip into the corners to make them lie flat.*

Frill edging

You will need enough extra backing fabric to cut strips for the frill. This type of finish can look very pretty on the edge of a cushion. The fabric for the frill needs to be light- to medium-weight fabric or it will be too bulky at the corners. Velvet is not suitable for this method.

1   First prepare the piece of embroidery for making up.
2   Cut a length of fabric on the straight of the grain at double the width you require the finished frill to be plus ½ in (13 mm) seam allowance on either edge. The length of the strip will depend on the type of gathers or pleats you wish to use, and can be joined if necessary. As a rough guide, allow between double and three times the length of the perimeter of the finished cushion.
3   Fold the strip in half so that the right side of the fabric is showing and the two raw edges are together. For a crisp folded edge, press the strip flat. For a softer fold, do not press. Tack the two edges together so that they do not move or come apart.
4   For a gathered frill use the largest machine stitch and slightly loosen the top thread tension. Stitch a row ¼ in (6 mm) below the stitching line and another ¼ in (6 mm) above. You could gather by hand along the same lines using a very long length of double sewing thread in the needle and working small running stitches. Then pull up the gathers, easing the fabric along so that the gathers are even and as full as you require. Pin the frill around the edge of the embroidery so that it faces inwards. Start at the centre point of the lower edge. You will have to adjust the gathers so that there is more fabric at the corners. This will ensure that you have pointed corners when the cushion cover is turned out.
5   For a pleated frill, start at the centre point of the lower edge and pleat the fabric up, pinning each pleat in place. If you want even pleats you will need to measure each one. When going around corners, allow more fabric so that when the cover is turned out the corners are not pulled in and squashed.
6   To join the frill turn in ½ in (13 mm) on either side of the join, cutting off any excess fabric. You will have to undo some of the tacking and gathering threads in order to do this. Then slipstitch the edges together. The join can be hidden in the gathers or pleats. Regather or pleat this little section and tack down again.
7   Continue making up as for a basic cushion.

Fastenings for cushions

It is not really necessary to have an opening with a fastening, since embroidered cushions need infrequent cleaning; when they do have to be cleaned the cushion must be taken apart. (See cleaning, page 103.) If you wish to have an opening, however, here are a few ways of doing it.

Zip along the edge of a cushion

1 Stitch any piping or frills on to the embroidered panel, following the instructions on pages 114–15 and 116.
2 The zip must be stitched along the lower edge and should be almost as long as the edge, so that the cushion pad can be easily inserted. Put the right side of the zip facing and the embroidery together, then pin, tack and machine (using the zipper/piping foot) on to the embroidered panel. Do the same with the backing.
3 Now pin, tack and machine around the rest of the cushion, leaving the zip open so that you can turn the cover out.
4 Turn the cover out, pull out the corners and insert the pad.

Zip down the back of the cushion

This is an easier method of inserting a zip. It does not have to go down the centre back; it could go diagonally or off-centre, and it could be made a feature if desired. You will need a zip that is 2 in (5 cm) shorter than the finished width or length (whichever way you require the zip) of the cushion.

1 Cut the backing of the cushion in two sections, allowing ¾ in (2 cm) for seam allowance on every edge.
2 Pin and tack together the seam where the zip is going to be inserted, then machine up the two ends, reversing the machine a couple of times at the point where it will join with the ends of the zip.
3 Pin and tack in the zip. The middle ridge of the zip should be aligned with the tacked-together seam. Machine in the zip using the zipper foot, then remove the tacking.
4 Continue to make up as for the basic cushion.

MAKING RUGS AND HANGINGS

Materials needed
Linen holland or similar hard-wearing fabric 2¼ in (6 mm) larger all round than the finished panel
Button thread

Only canvas work is really suitable for rugs, since it is hard-wearing. All types of embroidery can be made into hangings, however, whether small or large.

1 First prepare the piece of embroidery ready for making up.
2 Join the panels of embroidery if necessary.

(a) For canvas work, check that all the panels have the same number of stitches along the adjoining sides. If they are not the same, you will need to compensate by adding or unpicking rows. For other types of embroidery, measure the panels to ensure that they are the same size, trimming down any excess to a 1 in (2.5 cm) seam allowance, and making sure that the corners are right-angles.

(b) Pin the edges together. For canvas panels, place the pins about every ten stitches so that the panels match stitch for stitch. Pin only one edge of each panel at a time, or you will find it difficult to sew.

(c) Tack along the stitching line using a small, strong running stitch with double sewing thread in the needle.

(d) Now machine along these lines. Go along the seam several times to make it secure. For canvas work, machine slightly into the last row of stitches so that when the panels are flat no canvas shows.

(e) Repeat the tacking and machine stitching to join the other edges.

(f) Herringbone stitch back the seam allowances. For canvas work, the herringbone can go into the stitches on the back of the embroidery. For other types of embroidery, cut an interlining the size of the joined panels and place this on the wrong side of the embroidery. Flap the seam allowance over it and then herringbone it back on to the interlining. Remember to herringbone stitch back the seam allowance around the edge, too.

3   The complete panel may now need restretching. (See pages 99–100.)

4   To line the panel, lock stitch the interlining to the back of the panel down the centre and quarter lines, leaving a 2 in (5 cm) gap at the top and bottom. Now turn under the seam allowance on the lining and pin to the panel. The lining must be tight enough not to come forward but not so taut that it pulls on the panel, making it turn under.

5   To turn the panel into a hanging you will need to make slots along the top and bottom so that you can insert a pole for hanging. These slots must be added before the lining goes on.

(a) Cut two pieces of fabric about 4½ in (10 cm) wide or of a size appropriate to the size of the pole you intend to use. The length of the slot for the pole should be the width of the panel plus 2 in (5 cm). Turn in 1 in (2.5 cm) at each end and press. Then fold in half along the length, so that the folds are on the outside, and press again.

(b) Machine ¾ in (2 cm) up from the open edge to form a tube.

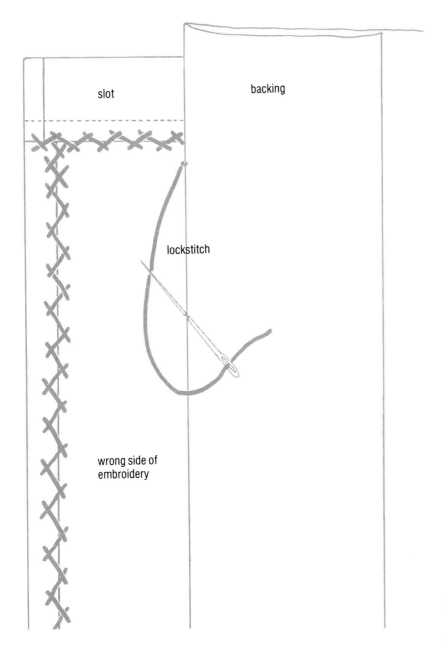

slot

backing

lockstitch

wrong side of
embroidery

Fig. 61 *Making a hanging. Use
herringbone to stitch back the seam
allowance, then stitch the slots in place,
then the backing. Lock stitch is used to
prevent the backing from dropping.*

(c) Lockstitch the folded edge of the slot on to the edge of the
panel, then herringbone stitch down the raw edge of the slot
on to the back of the embroidery.

(d) Stitch on the lining as for a rug.

(e) When the hanging is finished, the pole can be inserted into the
slot created.

BELL PULLS

The making up process for a bell pull is very similar to that for rugs and hangings except that you will have to purchase a pair of bell pull ends. These may already be in your kit, or many embroidery stockists will hold them.

1   First prepare the piece of embroidery ready for making up.
2   For techniques other than canvas work, cut a piece of interlining the size of the finished bell pull. This is then placed on the wrong side of the embroidery.
3   Trim down the excess fabric so that there is a 1 in (2.5 cm) seam allowance along the long edges and a 2 in (5 cm) allowance along the short ones.
4   Fold over the seam allowance along the longer sides and herringbone stitch down these edges to either the interlining or the back of the canvas stitches. Check that no canvas shows on the right side.
5   Now fold back the two shorter ends, encasing the bell pull ends. Herringbone stitch down along the raw edge.
6   Stitch on the lining, following the instructions for rugs and hangings on pages 118–19.
7   A cord could be added along the long sides, but this should be done before the lining is stitched on so that the ends are hidden by the lining.

HEMSTITCHING AND MITRED CORNERS

Hemstitching is an attractive way to finish off a piece of cross stitch that has been worked on an evenweave-type fabric and is going to be used as table linen. The corners should be mitred to give a neat finish. For cross stitch worked on aida, hemstitching can still be used, but omit the drawing out of the threads.

1   Cut the fabric to the required size and shape, allowing for the width of the hem plus ¼ in (6 mm) for turning. Make sure you cut the fabric on the straight of the grain; this can be done by following the threads of the fabric.
2   Measure up from the raw edges double the width of the required hem plus the turning allowance. Mark this point with a pin, and repeat on all four sides.
3   Snip through one or more threads of the fabric, depending on the size of the gap you want, at the point where the pin is. Using a tapestry needle, draw the threads back towards the corners where they meet, weave them back into the corner, then cut off the excess.

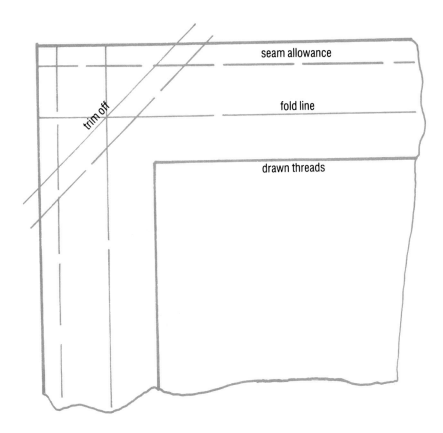

seam allowance

fold line

trim off

drawn threads

Fig. 62 *Making a mitred corner.*

4   Now turn the work over so that you have the wrong side uppermost. Press under the ¼ in (6 mm) seam allowance, then press the hem up so that the folded edge comes up to the drawn threads. It is very important that the hems are equal, or the mitred corners will be uneven. At the corners, press the hem straight across. These press lines will be used as guides for the mitred corners.

5   Unfold the corners and trim diagonally across the middle group of folds created by pressing the seams. Fold and press back the diagonal edges so that the fold intersects with the remaining crease at the corner. Now when the hem is turned up there should be a diagonal seam at the corners. This should be neatly oversewn in a sewing thread to match the background.

6   The hem can now be stitched down all the way round. To work hemstitch you can use either embroidery thread or a sewing thread in a matching or contrasting colour, in conjunction with a fine tapestry needle. Hemstitch is worked on the wrong side from left to right (right to left for left-handers). Start the thread off by coming through the fold and working a few small back stitches on the

crease. (See Fig. 63.) Come up through the hem two or three threads down at the point where you wish to start. Now take the needle around three or four of the drawn threads. These threads are pulled together by the working thread. Once you have chosen how many threads are to be pulled together and at what point on the hem, the number and position must be maintained throughout.

7   Continue by taking the needle back through the folded hem and along the remainder in the same way. To finish the thread off take the needle through the fold, working a few small back stitches to secure it, then cut off any excess.

Fig. 63 *Hemstitching. The same number of threads should be pulled together each time. A contrasting colour can be used to make a feature of it.*

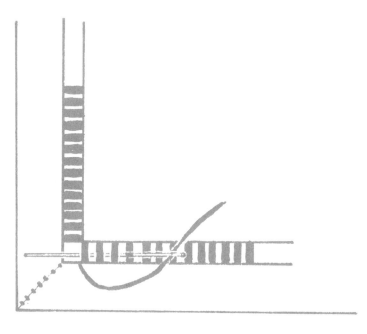

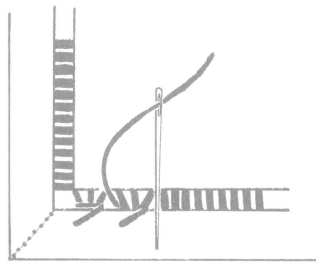

TASSELS

Tassels can make an interesting decoration on a cushion, bell pull or hanging. This method of making basic tassels is very simple. Tassels can be made out of one of the threads used in your embroidery, or you could use a contrasting thread.

1 Use a piece of card as a template so that your tassels match in length. To ensure a standard size, wrap the thread around the template counting the number of turns, or use exactly the same amount of thread – one skein, for example, each time.

2 Once you have wrapped enough thread around the template to create the required size of tassel, cut off any excess thread level with the base of the template at the starting point. Thread a large tapestry needle with a length of the same thread. Take this under the top edge of the wrapped threads, then tie a double knot. Remove the template and needle.

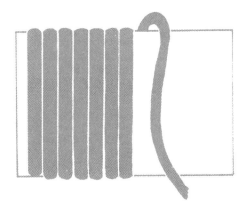

Fig. 64 *Wrapping the thread around a card template.*

3 To make the throat of the tassel, thread up your needle with another length of thread, either matching or contrasting. Holding the untied end of the tassel in your non-stitching hand, take the needle through the threads approximately one-third down the length of the tassel, leaving a 1 in (2.5 cm) end loose. Now tightly wrap the thread several times around the tassel at this point, making sure that you hold on to the end of the thread. Stitch through the throat of the tassel several times to finish it off, and cut off the excess working thread.

4 Cut through the threads at the end furthest from the throat. They will need to be neatened up; to do this, hold the ends between your fingers as if you were trimming hair. Use the lengths of thread you inserted earlier at the top of the tassel to attach it to your embroidery.

Fig. 65 *Making the throat of the tassel.*

CORDS

Simple twisted cords can be made for small objects such as pincushions. They should be reserved for small items, as it is not practical to make them in long lengths. You can use the same threads and colours as you used for the design, or contrasting ones. The thickness of the thread will determine the size of the cord, so to make a thicker cord you will need to add more threads.

1   Cut two lengths of thread three times longer than the finished cord length. Knot the two pieces together, so that the threads make a continuous loop.

2   Put one end over a secure hook or enlist the help of a friend. Using a pencil through the other end, pinch the thread together around the pencil and then twist the pencil. It is important to keep the thread taut at all times. If a friend is helping, get her to stand facing you and with a pencil through the end twist in the opposite direction.

3   When the thread has formed a tight twist put the two ends together, keeping the threads taut by holding the mid-point. If using a hook, loop the second end over the hook. If using a friend, give her your pencil to hold as well as her own. Starting at the mid-point, let go of a little of the cord at a time and it will twist together. If it does not twist together properly it is not tight enough, so more twisting is required. To make a two-coloured cord, instead of knotting together one colour use two and place the knots together midway between the two twisting points. To make a multi-coloured cord, knot together an even number of threads of the colours you wish to use and twist together as for the single colour. Unlike the regularity of the two-colour cord, however, the colours will come out randomly.

Further Information

BOOKS

Butler, Anne, *The Batsford Encyclopaedia of Embroidery Stitches*, B. T. Batsford, London 1979
Fifty Canvas Embroidery Stitches, J. & P. Coats Ltd, 1975
Thomas, Mary, *A Dictionary of Embroidery Stitches*, Hodder and Stoughton Ltd, London 1965

MAGAZINES

United Kingdom

Embroidery
Apartment 41
Hampton Court Palace
East Molesey
Surrey
KT8 9AU

Needlecrafts Magazine
Available bi-monthly from newsagents.

America

Just Cross Stitch
PO Box 420321
Palm Coast
FL 3142-0321

Needlepoint Plus
Box 54223
Boulder
CO 60322-4223

EMBROIDERY ASSOCIATIONS AND ORGANIZATIONS

United Kingdom

Embroiderers' Guild
Apartment 41
Hampton Court Palace
East Molesey
Surrey
KT8 9AU

Centre for Embroidery, Fashion and Textile Studies
66 New Bond Street
London W1

America

Embroiderers' Guild of America
335 West Broadway Suite 100
Louisville
KY 40202

American Needlepoint Guild
PO Box 241280
Memphis
TN 38124-1208

The National Academy of Needlearts
10300 Cherokee Road
Richmond
VA 23235

Index